BFI Film Classics

The BFI Film Classics is a series of books that introduces, interprets and celebrates landmarks of world cinema. Each volume offers an argument for the film's 'classic' status, together with discussion of its production and reception history, its place within a genre or national cinema, an account of its technical and aesthetic importance, and in many cases, the author's personal response to the film.

For a full list of titles available in the series, please visit our website: www.palgrave.com/bfi

'Magnificently concentrated examples of flowing freeform critical poetry.'
Uncut

'A formidable body of work collectively generating some fascinating insights into the evolution of cinema.'
Times Higher Education Supplement

'The series is a landmark in the history of film criticism.'
Quarterly Review of Film and Video

Editorial Advisory Board

Night of the Living Dead

Ben Hervey

A BFI book published by Palgrave Macmillan

© Ben Hervey 2008

First published in 2008 by
PALGRAVE MACMILLAN
Houndmills, Basingstoke, Hampshire RG21 6XS and
175 Fifth Avenue, New York, N.Y. 10010
Companies and Representatives throughout the world

on behalf of the

BRITISH FILM INSTITUTE
21 Stephen Street, London W1T 1LN
www.bfi.org.uk

There's more to discover about film and television through the BFI.
Our world-renowned archive, cinemas, festivals, films, publications and learning resources are
here to inspire you.

PALGRAVE MACMILLAN is the global academic imprint of the Palgrave Macmillan division of
St. Martin's Press, LLC and of Palgrave Macmillan Ltd. Macmillan® is a registered trademark in
the United States, United Kingdom and other countries.
Palgrave is a registered trademark in the European Union and other countries.

Reprinted 2008

Series cover design: Ashley Western
Series text design: ketchup/SE14

Set by D R Bungay Associates, Burghfield, Berkshire
Printed in China

This book is printed on paper suitable for recycling and made from fully managed and sustained
forest sources. Logging, pulping and manufacturing processes are expected to conform to the
environmental regulations of the country of origin.

British Library Cataloguing-in-Publication Data
A catalogue record for this book is available from the British Library

ISBN 978-1-84457-174-1

Contents

Acknowledgments

Thanks first to my parents, Tom and Carolyn Hervey, for all the expected reasons, and also for their thoughts on 1950s and 1960s America: they left for England, mainly for political reasons, right around the time that *Night of the Living Dead* began its midnight run at the Waverly.

The following were generous enough to share their knowledge and insights regarding *Night of the Living Dead*, its reception, its cultural contexts, and the sci-fi and horror genres: Barry N. Malzberg, Bill Landis and Michelle Clifford of Sleazoid Express, Elliott Stein, Rex Reed, Robert Mighall, Anton Bitel, Eddy Obermüller – and particularly Adam Lowenstein and Kim Newman, who also acted as first-class expert readers.

Peter Lurie first encouraged me to lecture on *Night of the Living Dead* at the University of Oxford. Said Marham of the Ultimate Picture Palace let me screen it for students at midnight. David Leake maintains the beautiful garden at Corpus Christi College, Oxford, where I wrote much of the manuscript.

At BFI Publishing I would like to thank Rob White, Rebecca Barden, Sarah Watt, Tom Cabot and Sophia Contento. Thanks also to the staff of the libraries where I researched this book: the Vere Harmsworth Library (Rothermere American Institute), the Bodleain Library, the BFI National Library (especially Sean Delaney), the New York Public Library and The Museum Library at The Museum of Modern Art, NYC (especially Charles Silver).

Thanks above all to my girlfriend Julia Markowski: despite her wholly unreasonable refusal to watch horror films, she has helped with every aspect of this undertaking, and still suffers dizzy spells at the mere mention of the New York Public Library microfilm readers.

Night of the Living Dead

Midnight Mass

It's a few minutes to midnight, any weekend in the summer of 1971. New York's Waverly Cinema is packed, and *Night of the Living Dead* is about to begin. Some chatter nervously: it's their first time watching a film that has been called the most terrifying ever made. But many of those waiting have seen *Night* many times, and know half the lines by heart: it has shown every Friday, Saturday and Sunday, only at midnight, since May. *Night* played at the Waverly for twenty-five weeks, then, after long, overlapping midnight runs at two other Manhattan cinemas, it returned, for fifty-five. The Waverly wasn't quite the first place to revive *Night* at midnight, but it was home, the

perfect spot for the cult to take root. The hippie musical *Hair*, then still in its first Broadway run, name-checked it as a bohemian meeting place.[1]

It was just round the corner from Washington Square, at the heart of Greenwich Village: then still a hub of the protest folk music scene, of gay liberation, avant-garde literature, the anti-war movement and the counterculture generally. The Waverly was three blocks from New York University. It was fifteen minutes' stroll from the site of Timothy Leary's LSD (League of Spiritual Discovery) Center, and barely ten from the Weather Underground safe house where three militant radicals blew themselves up in 1970, preparing to bomb a US Army dance. Greenwich Village was world-famous, synonymous with hip, intellectual, politicised youth.

The Waverly set the tone as *Night*'s midnight revival spread across America and Europe, and ran and ran through the 1970s. That the audiences were mostly young goes almost without saying: a 1968 MPAA survey found that viewers between sixteen and twenty-four accounted for half of the American box office, and far more for shocking, family-unfriendly films like *Night*. But the midnight movie phenomenon *celebrated* youth and rebellion: it was about staying up past bedtime, roaming the streets while regular citizens slept, and, usually, about defying good taste. Some films had been marginalised or vilified by the mainstream media. Those that played longest were often prized for transgressions and abnormality, like *Freaks* (1932) and *Pink Flamingos* (1972) (whose cannibal feast pays tribute to *Night*), or for anti-Establishment politics, like the anti-war freak-out *King of Hearts* (1966).

Night popularised midnight screenings but didn't start them. In the 1950s, midnight horror movies had been popular at Halloween; and through the 1960s, art houses occasionally showed underground films by the likes of Andy Warhol and Kenneth Anger after the regular programming. But the first feature to enjoy an extended, midnight-only run was Jodorowsky's lurid symbolist Western *El Topo* (1970), which opened at the Elgin, in New York's Chelsea, on 1 January 1971. The idea of the midnight 'cult' took shape with *El Topo*: the 'bearded and be-jeaned set' came ritually, week after week, memorising the lines and bringing new 'initiates'. *The Village Voice* called it 'Midnight Mass at the Elgin'; the fans were 'Jodorowsky's witnesses'. The cult grew by word-of-mouth: advertising was limited to a small box in the *Voice* (the Waverly did the same for *Night*). Drugs were used. The repeated viewings were all about 'getting' *El Topo*, interpreting its metaphors. Long conversations in cafés afterwards were part of the experience.

Night lacks *El Topo*'s metaphysical pretensions and overtly psychedelic visuals, but it was a surprisingly logical follow-up. It combined earlier midnight movie traditions and audiences: a horror movie that was also seen as an art film. Like *El Topo*, *Night* was a genre piece that bent its genre out of shape; both films were gory, broke taboos. Both, despite fantasy elements, felt shockingly '*real*', 'totally convincing': *El Topo*'s freakish actors were actually deformed; the underground press relished Jodorowsky's claim that he 'really raped' a girl for one scene. Both films were made outside Hollywood and the 'system'. And, like *El Topo*, *Night* was perceived to demand analysis, to work beneath the surface. Word had spread that it was an important, meaningful film, an urgent coded message on the state of America.[2]

I want to recapture *Night*'s significance for those early audiences: the ones who discovered it in the late 1960s, and the ones who made it a weekly ritual through the 1970s.

The Image Ten

Making an artistic statement was the last thing on the minds of George Romero and John Russo when they sat brooding in Samreny's Restaurant, Pittsburgh, in January 1967. They and a few friends had struggled for years to get into the movies, and had already dabbled in unconventional film-making. In 1960, they shot an experimental portmanteau comedy, *Expostulations*, but ran out of money in post-production; more recently, they had failed to launch *Whine of the Fawn*, a Bergman-esque drama about medieval religious conflicts. Romero had tried longest and hardest: he shot his first films at fourteen, and spent the summer before college, 1957, assisting on Hollywood sets. Since 1963, he, Russo and some friends had operated their own Pittsburgh-based advertising company, Latent Image, and were gradually getting known for leftfield, low-budget innovation. But Latent Image was always intended as a bridge to features. So over provolone sandwiches they resolved to make one for $6,000, with ten investors kicking in $600 apiece. This time they'd play it safe with an exploitation picture. Their unpretentious working title: *Monster Flick*.

Assembling the rest of the 'Image Ten' was easy, and all provided services too. Four were Romero and Russo's partners at Latent Image, including Russ Streiner, who produced, and Vince Survinski, production director. Karl Hardman and Marilyn Eastman worked in advertising elsewhere, and handled *Night*'s music and sound.

After several false starts, Romero showed up with half a story inspired by *I Am Legend* (1954), Richard Matheson's novel about the last human in a world of vampires. Romero preferred to show the beginning of the undead's takeover. The novel had already been filmed in Italy as *The Last Man on Earth* (1964), starring Vincent Price, and prefigured key details of *Night*: slow-moving hordes, hands grasping through boarded windows, an infected child on her deathbed, mounds of burning corpses – plus the protagonist dies. *Last Man* deserves more recognition, but lacks the qualities that made *Night* a hit: its rawness, brutality and grinding naturalism; its assault on taboos and cherished values; its queasy black humour and its topicality.

Six thousand dollars was not nearly enough, and the Image Ten eventually found additional investors. But they economised resourcefully. After months spent scouring Pittsburgh's environs, they rented an Evans City farmhouse: it was due to be bulldozed,

Undead hordes, boarded windows: *The Last Man on Earth* (1964)

The Evans City
farmhouse

so they could do as much damage as they wanted. (As it happened, the
boarded-up farmhouse stood for years to come, crowded with dummy
ghouls and corpses, fodder for local kids' nightmares.) They lived there
during the shoot, partly to guard the equipment. There was no running
water, so they bathed in the creek and carried buckets from the spring.
They slept on army surplus cots; after Romero's tore, he used the floor.
But they usually only managed a few hours' sleep anyway: they filmed
around their day-jobs, on weekends, holidays and by night.

Eight of the Image Ten appeared in the film, some in major roles:
Streiner played Johnny, Hardman and Eastman were the Coopers.
The remaining cast were mainly friends, colleagues, clients and local
volunteers. Only Judith O'Dea (Barbara[3]) and Duane Jones (Ben) were
even part-time professional actors, and neither had done a feature.
The special effects were strictly DIY, with clay for rotting flesh and
ping-pong ball eyes; the blood was Bosco chocolate syrup. (Romero
worried that it would show up brown when *Night* was colourised for
video.) The film-makers were so set on wringing 'production value'
from anything to hand that they wrote in Barbara's car crash because
Streiner's mother had dented her car shopping. This determination
extended to dangerous stunts: Russo set himself on fire for the Molotov
cocktail scene. The same recklessness energised post-production:

Streiner got their final mix and sound-lock for free by beating the lab boss at a double-or-nothing chess game.

Night was shot mostly in sequence, which helps to explain why its intensity and bleakness build throughout – and perhaps why its subtexts emerge more in later scenes. The story continued to form during shooting: Romero only half-scripted it before they started. Russo helped write the remainder, and others threw in ideas. The same applied on set: everyone helped with make-up, lighting, set-dressing. At this distance, it's impossible to disentangle who did what or had which idea, so I will speak of 'the Image Ten' or 'the film-makers' when a decision wasn't clearly Romero's. Indeed, Romero wasn't even chosen to direct until pre-production was well under way. Nonetheless, *Night* is his film more than anyone else's, and he ended up doing more than most 'auteurs'. Besides conceiving the story, co-scripting and directing, he handled all of the camerawork and editing, acted (briefly), designed make-up and lighting effects and had final say on music and sound.

He took his time. The Image Ten's situation was highly unusual: they made *Night* without a deadline and owned their equipment.

Ordinary effects: note the tub of Bosco chocolate syrup

Everyone worked without counting the hours, especially Romero, a notorious perfectionist, who reportedly put in twenty-four-hour days editing. He cultivated a remarkably labour-intensive style. In ninety-six minutes, *Night* contains nearly eleven hundred cuts: very brisk by contemporary Hollywood standards, but almost surreal for a palpably micro-budgeted film. Much of *Night*'s unique feel comes from this bewildering collision of low-budget resources and high-budget man-hours. It's the same with the music: it's all public domain stuff, from library discs, but Hardman and Eastman synchronised it better than most custom-written scores.

Shooting lasted nine months, post-production five. The finished product didn't quite meet Hollywood standards of transparent professionalism. *Night* has some minor rough edges, like continuity and screen direction lapses, which I won't dwell on, because they don't hurt it. It also has arguably major ones, like the limitations of the camera and actors, on which I will dwell, because I think they enhance the film's effect. But *Night* was a real movie, made by unknowns in Pittsburgh of all places, without studio help, for $114,000 (half deferred until after release). And it was taken seriously and became an international hit. Besides *Night*'s vast artistic significance, it was a shake-up for the industry, a blow to Hollywood supremacy and a lasting inspiration for regional and independent film-makers: without it, Quentin Tarantino says, 'you probably wouldn't have Steven Soderbergh'.[4]

From the drive-ins to MOMA

Rumour has it that *Night* remains, by tickets sold, the most successful independent film, and near the top for the horror genre: it stayed in theatrical distribution for almost a decade, and has never lapsed from print on video. We will never know. The Image Ten waited in vain for documentation and royalties from *Night*'s revival shows and foreign runs. They sued the distributor, Continental, but the case limped on for years inconclusively, until Continental's parent company, the Walter Reade Organization, filed

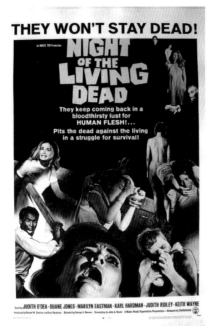

for bankruptcy. The rights reverted to the film-makers in time for the home video boom, but they faced another hitch. *Night* changed titles twice after completion: it was *Night of Anubis*, then *Night of the Flesh Eaters*, until the producers of *The Flesh Eaters* threatened legal action. In the hurry to substitute the final title card, the copyright declaration was omitted, and *Night* entered the public domain: bootlegs (usually from 16mm prints) are ubiquitous. But it's not just the figures: even the broad contours of *Night*'s release have become shrouded in myth. It's worth a moment to set the record at least relatively straight.

The Image Ten rightly regretted signing with Continental, but the move may have helped *Night*'s cult appeal. The other interested distributors were Columbia and American International Pictures (AIP). With Columbia's logo spliced on front, *Night* would have lost some underground mystique. AIP, past the glory days of Corman's Poe series, were increasingly regarded as conservative hacks: *inter/VIEW*, whose praise proved crucial in making *Night* hip, meanwhile ran articles on 'The Decline of AIP'. Besides, AIP demanded a happy ending, and *Night*'s refusal to compromise is at the heart of its success. Continental accepted *Night* almost unchanged: they wanted a little less talk and more gore. They weren't scared by controversy: they had already released films that had been refused Production Code seals and condemned by the Legion of Decency. And their attachment left *Night*'s cultural standing valuably ambiguous: they had distributed horror and sci-fi, but were better known for serious imports like *Room at the Top* (1959); Walter Reade also owned a successful art-house chain.[5]

Continental's art-house sensibilities probably made them more receptive to *Night*, but they didn't understand what they had. They toured twelve prints around the drive-in and exploitation circuit with *Dr Who and the Daleks* (1965), preceded by hackneyed ads promising '$50,000 if you die of fright!'. Yet *Night* performed excellently, breaking records at many venues. The National Association of Theater Owners selected it as 'exploitation picture of the month'.

Reviews were mixed. In the *New York Times*, Vincent Canby dismissed *Night* as a 'grainy little movie' with 'nonprofessional actors', a 'wobbly camera' and 'hollow' sound. Continental's penny-pinching was partly to blame: *Night*'s negative is beautifully lit, with sharp detail and contrast, but their slipshod prints, as Lee Beaupre complained in *Variety*, resembled '20-year-old Army stock'. Like Canby, Beaupre lambasted *Night* for 'amateurism of the first order', but that was the least of it:

Until the Supreme Court establishes clear-cut guidelines for the pornography of violence, 'Night of the Living Dead' will serve quite nicely as an outer-limit definition by example. In a mere 90 minutes, this horror film (pun intended) casts serious aspersions on the integrity and social responsibility of its Pittsburgh-based makers, distrib Walter Reade, the film industry as a whole and exhibs who book the pic, as well as raising doubts about the future of the regional cinema movement and about the moral health of filmgoers who cheerfully opt for this unrelieved orgy of sadism.

Robert Ebert watched the film at a Saturday matinee packed with young children. *Night*'s violence and bleakness left them stunned and weeping:

they'd seen some horror movies before, sure, but this was something else. This was ghouls eating people up – and you could actually see what they were eating. This was little girls killing their mothers. ... Worst of all, even the hero got killed.

Ebert has been mocked for his write-up, but it was an attack on negligent exhibitors and parents, not on *Night*. Anyway, it was great publicity: *Reader's Digest* reprinted it and made *Night* notorious. Other notices were favourable – the *Film and Television Daily* called *Night* a 'gem', with 'all the earmarks of a "sleeper"' – but they treated it simply as an effective shocker.[6] That changed in late 1969, when Continental reissued *Night* with *Slaves* (1969). Herbert Biberman's ante-bellum drama about cruel white plantation owners and noble black slaves had underwhelmed *Variety* but delighted European intellectuals: *Positif* gave it half an issue.

The fourth issue of (fellow Pittsburgher) Andy Warhol's new magazine, *inter/VIEW*, reviewed *Night twice*, alongside a substantial Romero interview, and named it in several best-of-year lists. Reviewer George Abagnalo, later a Warhol scriptwriter, perhaps did more than anyone else to turn the critical tide:

Frequently an artistic film containing nudity will play the nudie theatre circuit. Cinema-sophisticates see it at an art house and understand and appreciate it, while voyeurs see it on 42nd Street and don't care what it's really about.

Night's gore 'made it eligible for 42nd Street', he argued, but it was time to recognise 'the work of art it really is': 'It should open at an art house and run for at least a month, because it is a work of art.' Richard McGuinness took up the cause in the last *Village Voice* of the 1960s (dated Christmas day, 1969), nagging New York's Museum of Modern Art to show it. Elliott Stein, who reviewed *Night* for *Sight and Sound* in early 1970, was more proactive. He dragged MOMA curators Adrienne Mancia and Larry Kardish eleven blocks downtown to watch the film in an authentic 42nd Street fleapit, its natural habitat.[7] *Night* was still packing those grindhouses when MOMA announced its screening. It was held the following June, in a season showcasing new auteurs. Romero, still visibly surprised, took questions from a standing-room-only crowd.[8]

   Night's improving critical fortunes emboldened Continental to release it internationally that spring. According to Rex Reed, it was translated into twenty-five languages. British prints were cripplingly censored, but *Night* drew huge crowds in France, Spain and Italy. Madrid's largest cinema reportedly ran it for eighteen months, and it was re-released to French cinemas as recently as 2006. European critics, doubtless apprised of American developments (some quoted *inter/VIEW*), received it warmly. Highbrow publications like *Sight and Sound* and *Positif* were particularly effusive, but even most newspaper critics judged it a terrifying, intelligent, meaningful film.

Night and the intellectuals

ROMERO   I wrote Night ... as a short story, which strangely enough was an allegorical thing, but then when we did the film, the allegory went out. But not entirely ...

ARTHUR   The Europeans picked up on the allegory.

Andy Warhol's Interview, 1973[9]

As *Night* became a cult, its original release was mythologised. Arthur Rubine, Romero's press agent and formerly director of

Walter Reade, tagged along for Romero's second encounter with
the renamed *Andy Warhol's Interview* and reshuffled history.
Since then the received wisdom, which even Romero repeats, is that
Night 'was basically discovered by the French'. The first American
release did only decent business, and all the critics hated it. But the
Europeans understood: *Sight and Sound* and *Cahiers du cinéma*
'went ape'. Rex Reed supposedly read about *Night* in *Cahiers*, or
even watched it among Parisian cinephiles, and brought word back
home – and so to the *Slaves* re-release, *inter/VIEW*, MOMA,
Stateside recognition and packed midnight shows. Not so: Serge
Daney's *Cahiers* review was surprisingly negative, and Reed didn't
read it, let alone see *Night* in Paris (anyway, he didn't mention *Night*
in print until the Waverly revival began). Even Elliott Stein was a
New Yorker, albeit one who lived mainly in Paris as a *Financial
Times* correspondent. Americans, notably Warhol's crowd,
'discovered' *Night* first.[10]

The myth sidesteps one of the most significant aspects of
Night's progress: it was rehabilitated as 'art' while still drawing
exploitation crowds at grindhouses and drive-ins. As Abagnalo
acknowledged, it was relatively common for art-house fare by
Bergman or Warhol to play grindhouses too if it showed some skin.
But it was new, at least in America, for a film to cross over so rapidly
the other way. *Night* probably did as much to dismantle cultural
hierarchies as Leslie Fiedler and Susan Sontag. Its simultaneous
highbrow/lowbrow status set the tone for 1970s midnight screenings,
where Cocteau rubbed shoulders with Ed Wood, Junior.

But the myth's popularity says a lot about how cult audiences
wanted to perceive *Night*. Rubine, who also handled publicity for
films by Fellini, Malle and Truffaut, cannily presented it almost as a
daring European import. He knew that even (or especially) in the
States, *Night* found its core audience among those who were
sceptical of the American mainstream, politically and culturally.
It became a badge of honour that *Night* had been spurned by
Hollywood's cronies at *Variety*, the family-values middlebrows at

Reader's Digest. As for Canby, he slated *El Topo*. *Night*'s cult boomed at a time when ads for Antonioni's *Zabriskie Point* (1970) and Andy Warhol's novel *a* trumpeted damning reviews from mainstream organs like the *New York Times*. *Night*'s supposedly blanket first-run rejection by straight American philistines perfectly complemented its outsider status: its tiny budget, regional origins and untutored style. The Image Ten did their own thing; naturally the Establishment didn't like it.

Rubine's version exaggerated a nonetheless fundamental truth: that *Night*'s intellectual rehabilitation preceded and informed its peak of popularity. Second-run viewers turned up expecting *Night* to be 'more terrifying than Hitchcock's "Psycho"!', but also *art*, a statement. Programme notes were distributed at some campus screenings, quoting *Sight and Sound* and academic journals. Midnight crowds watched through the prism of intellectuals' responses.

I'll refer throughout to what contemporary critics saw in *Night*. Almost all praised its self-aware subversion of generic cliché, and its uncompromising, unrelieved brutality and bleakness, particularly its shock ending. Many linked these qualities with *Night*'s gritty, raw texture: for second-run reviewers, the non-professional feel that Canby scorned actually enhanced *Night*'s genre-defying realism.

The monochrome was key. Following a decade of Hammer and AIP Gothics in widescreen and Technicolor, *Night* was almost the last horror film to be released in old-fashioned Academy ratio black and white. But its visual plainness ironically made it feel *more* contemporary: it became a gimmick in itself. Colour was already the norm, but film-makers sometimes preferred black and white for grim social realism or true stories, like *In Cold Blood* (1967) and *The Battle of Algiers* (1966): it tapped authenticity from decades of black-and-white newsreels, documentaries and television news broadcasts. Says Romero: 'In those days the news was in black-and-white. Black-and-white was the medium. It was much more realistic back then.'[11]

Usually a recklessly honest interviewee, he got carried away and told *inter/VIEW* that he used it 'by choice. We could have had the budget for color.' Word spread. (Sixteen-millimetre colour *was* mooted partway through production, but immediately rejected: it would have meant extensive reshoots, and everyone worried that the 35mm blow-up would render the picture quality unreleasable.[12])

Second-run reviewers loved the monochrome, the 'wobbly' camera, the TV-shaped frame. Perhaps even Continental's dingy prints helped *Night*'s reappraisal. Critics differed over how much credit they gave the film-makers: Europeans were generally quicker to recognise Romero's craftsmanship, while some early American reviews treated it rather patronisingly, almost as naive folk art. Pauline Kael, who judged *Night* 'one of the most gruesomely terrifying films ever made', backhandedly enthused about its 'flat' acting and 'grainy, banal seriousness': 'there's no art to transmute the ghoulishness'.[13] But all agreed that *Night*'s rawness made it more frightening and convincing. It complemented the drab, middle-of-nowhere locations, the store-bought clothes, the authentically unglamorous Pittsburghers: *au fait* with Warhol and Pasolini, highbrow critics mostly saw *Night*'s non-professional actors as a plus. This wasn't Hollywood gloss: it felt *real*. Many used words like 'documentary' and 'newsreel' to describe *Night*'s style: it helped connect the film to contemporary realities.

Rubine is partly right: European journals did more to 'discover'*Night* as a topical, political film. For Richard McGuinness, in *The Village Voice*, what set *Night* apart was its reduction of the horror genre to its cruel, nihilistic core, remorselessly purging every extraneous cliché, frill, comfort and 'metaphysic-implying obfuscation'. McGuinness's approach recalls 1960s criticism on pop art and minimalism. *Night* was art by dint of single-minded purity: a horror film as austerely definitive, as flatly iconic as Warhol's silkscreens of Marilyn, soup tins ... and race riots. Similar concerns underlie the *inter/VIEW* coverage. Both magazines acknowledged the significance of the posse scenes and Ben's death, but didn't probe *Night*'s politics much further.

Stein's *Sight and Sound* review established themes that have dominated discussion ever since: racism, the breakdown of the American family, and the resurgence of political conservatism. He subtly invoked Vietnam: 'Who are these ghouls, who are these saviours, all of them so horrifying, so convincing, who mow down, *defoliate* and gobble up everything in their path?' (my emphasis). It's a fittingly iconoclastic review. Stein was friendly with fellow ex-pat William Burroughs and had just co-written and performed in Antony Balch's lurid erotic horror film *Secrets of Sex* (1970).

French and British intellectuals pounced on these subtexts. In *Positif*, Ado Kyrou described the posse: 'the lynchers, the witch-hunters … let off steam by shooting the monsters that they have spawned … it's less dangerous than Vietnam and just as exciting'. Kyrou considered *Night* 'un film politique', thinly disguised as a (very effective) horror movie: he, Stein, Daney and even mainstream European reviewers read the whole film as an allegory, not just the ending. Their response was not entirely surprising. Many influential French *cinéphiles* seemed to like nothing better than exhilaratingly violent, all-American pop culture that could also be read as a critique of American malaise: witness *Cahiers*' raptures over *Kiss Me, Deadly* (1955). Yet Vincent Canby, obviously piqued, singled out Stein's *Night* review in a *New York Times* think-piece decrying film criticism's new decadence: the dismaying eagerness, even among Anglophone writers, to find profound meanings in offensive trash. If anything, the currents of change ran deeper than Canby realised. Those reviews paved the way for full-blown interpretive articles and academic criticism, which began, courtesy of Dillard and Robin Wood, with *Night*'s midnight shows still in theatres. And more grassroots, anecdotal fanzine pieces on *Night* and its audiences show that metaphor-hunting was very much part of the experience even for paying customers.[14]

1968

It was 1968, man. *Everybody* had a message.

George Romero[15]

Political readings were almost inevitable. *Night* was released in an
infamous year for the United States, when tensions that had built
over several years erupted in fire and blood: 1968 unreeled like one
long horror film, without logic, explanation or happy ending.
The shocks kicked off in January with the Tet Offensive, a surprise
North Vietnamese and Vietcong attack on over one hundred South
Vietnamese towns and cities. Tet brought unprecedentedly disturbing
images to primetime television, most notoriously South Vietnam's
chief of police offhandedly shooting a suspected Vietcong captive
point blank: 'Shoot'em in the head,' as *Night*'s posse-leader says.
American presence in Vietnam escalated sharply through 1967, and
when news of Tet broke, the Joint Chiefs of Staff demanded 206,000
more men. As 1968 began, America's young were likelier than ever
to be drafted, and the war looked even more dangerous, futile and
sickening than before. In March, frenzied American troops massacred
over three hundred civilians, mostly women and children, at My Lai.
The army managed to cover it up until November 1969, proving
themselves conmen as well as butchers.

Meanwhile, schisms back home seemed to teeter near civil war.
Anti-war and anti-Establishment activity reached a desperate pitch.

Fifty thousand
demonstrators had
marched on the
Pentagon in October
1967. Through March
and April of 1968,
student protestors
occupied buildings at
Columbia University.
The police removed

Photo: Eddie Adams, 1968

them violently. That spring, it felt like a repressive crackdown had begun. Progressive figures, notably Martin Luther King and anti-war presidential nominee candidate Robert Kennedy, were assassinated in still-mysterious circumstances. King's death sparked bloody race riots throughout America, even worse than those that hit over a hundred cities in 1967, while the Image Ten shot *Night*. Black leaders renounced non-violent protest. Five weeks before *Night* premiered, the Chicago police gassed and billy-clubbed peaceful demonstrators outside the 1968 Democratic Convention. By November, it seemed like the warmongers had won: Nixon was elected president by what he called America's 'Silent Majority' of patriotic conservatives.

Before *Night* opened at the Waverly, America had watched the 1960s' gory death throes. Hippie ideals were irremediably tarnished when Manson family commune members were convicted of the Tate–LaBianca murders. The Beatles-fixated longhairs stabbed their victims dozens of times each and cut an eight-month foetus from Sharon Tate's womb: an orgy of bodily destruction more crazed than *Night*'s cannibal feast. In May 1970, following America's invasion of Cambodia, the National Guard opened fire on protestors at Kent State University, killing four and wounding nine. Several were shot in the back. Ten days later, the police fired on students at Jackson State University. Suddenly, peace protestors had to be willing to risk their *lives*.

The morning after the Robert Kennedy assassination, his

speechwriter Arthur Schlesinger broadcast his thoughts on America: 'We are today the most frightening people on the planet.' Little wonder, then, that young viewers responded to a brutally violent horror film set

Outside the 1968 Democratic Convention: a government-appointed commission called it a 'police riot'

here and now, which scrapped the genre's foreign or alien threats and pitted Americans against Americans. Little wonder that its moral ambiguity felt true to them, its refusal to idolise heroes or demonise monsters, or to rejoice when order and normality prevail.

The accidental classic?

A lot of the critics have jumped off the deep end in likening the ghouls to the silent majority and finding all sorts of implications that none of us ever intended. I think George wants to encourage that kind of thinking on the part of some critics. But I'd rather tell them they're full of shit.

John Russo, 1975[16]

INTERVIEW Was that a formula with the black hero?
ROMERO It was an accident. The whole movie was an accident.[17]

The turbulent late 1960s mostly found Hollywood at its fluffiest and most escapist. Vietnam was off limits, except for John Wayne, who made *The Green Berets* (1968) with Lyndon Johnson's blessing and massive Defense Department assistance. The result was as morally uncomplicated as, the producer told *Variety*, 'Cowboys and Indians. ... The Americans are the good guys and the Viet Cong are the bad guys.'[18] Hollywood's racial message films were barely less trite and anachronistic. Young and politically engaged viewers must have been desperate to see films that grappled with their era's turmoil, or at least acknowledged it – and preferably without contrived preachiness and moral uplift. Did that desperation make them read too much into *Night*?

Russo and other Image Ten members said so back then, but their remarks should be seen in perspective. They were understandably disgruntled that the same cinephiles who interpreted *Night* also championed Romero as 'auteur' and marginalised his collaborators. Early interviews find Romero rather taken aback by highbrow responses and experimenting with his own opinions, but I don't believe that he has merely played along with critics, as Russo suggests. It's likelier that Romero simply saw more in *Night* than Russo did, and that his understanding grew in retrospect – hardly unusual. It *was* more his creation than anyone else's, and he has developed its themes in excellent, thoughtful work, particularly his sequels *Dawn of the Dead* (1978), *Day of the Dead* (1985), *Land of the Dead* (2005) and *Diary of the Dead* (2007) and his 1970s films, such as *Martin* (1977) and *The Crazies* (1973). The other Image Ten members have mostly dropped out of features. Russo has remained more active, notably with *Midnight* (1981) and latterly with the likes of *Santa Claws* (1996) ('His SLAY BELLS are ringing!'). His novel *Return of the Living Dead* spawned Dan O'Bannon's popular 1985 film adaptation and a parallel series of *Night* sequels. Even Russo's better work, though, aspires to little more than straight-ahead scares and chuckles, and his butchered twenty-fifth anniversary edition of *Night*, with its inane substitute music and newly shot footage, travesties everything that makes the original special.

But Romero's 'accident' remark, flippant and exaggerated as it was, warrants serious consideration. Some elements that excited critics *were* fortuitous: that Ben is black, for example, and the ghouls and posse all white. Key factors of the 'vérité' style were budget-imposed: the real locations, unknown cast and monochrome. Before I 'jump off the deep end' myself, I need to clarify and justify my approach.

First, *Night* is not merely the product of its film-makers' intentions, even if we pretend that they all shared the same ones. *Night*, even more than most films, is what it has become: that includes 'accidents', improvisations and even critics' interpretations, which have so conditioned viewing as to become almost inextricable. And, as I've said, a large part of my goal is to recreate what *Night* meant to viewers then. What I won't attempt is to force it into a single, coherent allegory (the ghouls mean this, *ergo* Ben means that and the posse means the other): futile when the film-makers clearly didn't structure it as one.

That said, I do not believe that critics and audiences merely dreamed up *Night*'s subtexts. There were accidental factors, but the

film, even the script, formed with those factors in place. Saddled with
black and white, Romero shot and cut to enhance the rough,
spontaneous, almost documentary feel. 'We make a living making a
glass of beer look like heaven,' he explained: 'Maybe that's why we
went as far the other way as we did.' He deliberately chose
unsuitable, over-grainy stock for some scenes.[19] Even the television
news broadcasts were written in with the black and white in place,
and inevitably brought home the 'newsreel' style of the rest.

Newsreel style doesn't necessarily entail newsreel relevance.
But Romero has always said that he shot the posse scenes and the
ending with politics consciously in mind; and for Jones, the whole film
was always political. Some details, we'll see, were clearly meant to be
topical, like the 'Search and Destroy' segment. Romero's position now,
which even Russo and the others seem to have accepted, is that even
though they did not intend *Night* as one big statement, politics was
always on their minds. Romero says that he originally conceived the
story as an allegory, and they went on interpreting it during the shoot:
'We lived in that farmhouse. ... And we sat around and we talked a lot
about the themes that were in the film, the disintegration of the family
unit and the idea of revolution and all that stuff.'[20] But *Night*'s
implications hit audiences more powerfully for not being laboured
over: they're genuine subtexts. If the film had been constructed as a

vehicle for political rhetoric, it would have turned out flat, obvious and inflexible: not just rooted in its era, but shackled to it.

Finally, there's one fundamental issue on which everyone agreed from the start: realism. As Streiner put it: 'deep down inside we were all serious filmmakers and somewhat disappointed because we had to resort to horror'. They resolved, at least, to make *Night* 'real and true' (Russo's words), to give it an honesty lacking from other 'monster flicks'.[21] Can realism ever be ideologically detached, self-contained, let alone in the late 1960s? Consider what was 'real and true' for the Image Ten: untrustworthy television news broadcasts, a military–governmental conspiracy to keep dangerous secrets from the public, the failure of good intentions, a murdered black hero. *Night*'s realism reflects a specific worldview: late 1960s liberalism souring into cynicism. Romero says that he and his fellow film-makers were 'part of that liberal gang – hippies who didn't want to grow up'.[22] He had dropped out of college to lead a bohemian, nocturnal, pot-smoking life,[23] and like most of his collaborators he was still on the trustworthy side of thirty. *Night* was something new: a genre film made by politically engaged young people without the older generation looking over their shoulder, whether Hollywood studio bosses or the equally conservative businessmen who ran Hammer and AIP.

'Scenes we'd like to see'

Mad Magazine ran a regular feature through the 1960s and 1970s, 'Scenes we'd like to see': the hero chickens out and leaves the damsel tied to the tracks; the Joker kills Robin across town while Batman changes a flat; the lion eats Dorothy. *Mad* deflated movie clichés with harsh realities: people can turn cowardly and sneaky or make mistakes; accidents happen. *Night* does the same.[24] In pursuit of authenticity and truth, it debunked everything that had served to vanquish evil in prior 'monster flicks': individual heroism, teamwork, science, knowledge, religion, love, the family, the media, the army and the government. Panic, selfishness and power struggles tear the would-be heroes apart before the ghouls do. We never quite find out what is going on. And everyone dies, usually ingloriously, even by accident. Much has been made, and rightly, of how disturbing these transgressions are, but, as *Mad*'s title points out, we *want* to see them: they are also liberatingly honest and even funny.

Where did the Image Ten find the clichés they upturned? Although everyone now files *Night* under horror, contemporary critics more often saw it in the context of apocalyptic sci-fi, naming titles from the 1950s and early 1960s. The Image Ten's initial Monster Flick concept was a 1950s sci-fi pastiche that took the aliens' side against ridiculous 'authority figures' like 'Sheriff Suck'. In some ways, that's not *so* far from the film they made. They grew up on 1950s sci-fi. Romero's first juvenile short was *The Man from the Meteor*. Russo claims that 'as a kid' he saw 'just about every' monster and sci-fi film of the 1950s and early 1960s,[25] and while it's possible to identify films with specific similarities (*Day the World Ended* [1955], *Invisible Invaders* [1959], *Panic in Year Zero!* [1962]), *Night* feels like the product of watching *all* of them, as if it's moulded from the generic mulch they left in the mind: experiments gone wrong, radiation from outer space, dead-eyed humans stripped of individuality, conferences between soldiers and scientists, well-behaved young lovers, bald patriarchs, TV bulletins, windowless

Invisible Invaders (1959)

basements, survivalist strategising, the end of the world. *Night* even looks and sounds 1950s. It's in Academy ratio black and white, like most 1950s sci-fi. Some of *Night*'s decades-old library music had shown up in 1950s schlock like *Teenagers from Outer Space* (1959) and *The Hideous Sun Demon* (1959). Many elements of *Night* were familiar, but its originality comes partly from twisting the familiar into something radically new, subverting and inverting the expectations it sets up. It's a jarring mix of nostalgia and iconoclasm.

And perhaps that mix is also what *Night*'s audiences felt when they looked back at the 1950s: these were their childhood years too, and must naturally have evoked at least *some* fond nostalgia. But they also represented everything that the rebellious younger generation wanted to interrogate, upturn, transcend and escape. The term 'fifties' has an almost intrinsically mythological ring when applied to America, partly because it usually denotes a way of life and set of attitudes that overhung the decade, but more because it conjures an idealised image of domestic life: a collage of grinning suburban tableaux from sitcoms, leisure magazines and home appliance adverts, beguiling but phoney and stifling. The 1962 Port Huron Statement, generally considered the opening shot of student radicalism, starts by evoking an idealised America 'when we were kids', then punctures that cosy nostalgia: 'the hypocrisy of American ideals was discovered ... we began to sense that what we had originally seen as the American Golden Age was actually the decline of an era'.[26] I want to argue that, besides its relevance to 1960s issues like Vietnam, *Night*'s sceptical engagement with 1950s myths and iconography proved perversely crucial in making it feel so contemporary.

Night connects back to the core theme of Gothic literature and film: the enlightened present's struggle to overcome a barbarous past, whether in the form of feudal despots and Catholic inquisitors or centuries-old vampires and living mummies. But which represents the past in *Night*: the resurrected dead, or the normality that they threaten to tear apart?

Nostalgia and iconoclasm: when a film becomes a cult, when fans watch it ten and twenty times, it is inevitably no longer just about the shock of the new, but also the pleasures of the familiar. Transgression, killing the past, becomes a ritual.

The clock strikes twelve, the curtains part ...

'You used to really be scared here'

Fade up to a deep-focus shot of a winding country road, static as a painting. A car rounds the furthest bend, half a mile distant, snaking our way. *Night* will become inexorably more claustrophobic, squeezing its characters into smaller spaces (a house, a few boarded-up rooms, a windowless basement) and sweatier, more frantically edited close-ups. So it makes sense to start at the opposite extreme, with the film's most languid, expansive landscape shot, almost agoraphobic in its sense of remoteness. Nudging forty seconds, this is also (bar the television broadcasts) *Night*'s longest unbroken take. It leaves room for the loneliness to sink in. The car leaves two straggling houses far behind and, in the slow montage that follows, no possible destination looms, not a living soul: just muddy slopes, bare trees and lopsided pylons dwindling to the vanishing point: deepest nowhere. As the title comes up, 'living dead' seems apt to describe the half-life evoked by this Middle American wilderness. At last a ravaged signpost marks the cemetery; it looks full of bullet holes, foreshadowing the violence to come.

Night's credit sequence is oddly haunting, conjuring the mundane terrors of loneliness and isolation that underpin the film's more visceral scares. Seemingly, it caught Kubrick's eye. *The Shining*'s (1980) credits are *Night* souped-up: the winding, tree-lined road to nowhere; the lonely car; the familiar music made strange by electronics. Hardman and Eastman often used simple, judicious studio effects to make *Night*'s stock music their own: speed changes, feedback loops. Here the effect is subtle, lulling and oneiric, like an audio equivalent of the focus shimmers that cue flashback scenes. This isn't quite the 1950s, but a hazy dream of them: Romero called

Night's music 'the scoring heard in nightmares conjured by yesterday's matinees'.[27] It's just right to bring out the old-timiness of that TV-shaped, black-and-white picture. Nervous apprehension probably mingled with disarming cosiness as midnight audiences settled into these credits, as if snuggling up for a late-night *Twilight Zone* rerun.

Romero's director credit appears over the Stars and Stripes, fluttering above the headstones – and waving goodbye to the vague, timeless Middle European settings of the Universal–Hammer Gothic tradition. *Night* is about America; even Romero's apocalyptic sequels never mention events elsewhere.

The car pulls up and Barbara looks out: 'They ought to make the day the time changes the first day of summer.' Her words peg this for high spring. In fact, the graveyard opening was the last scene to be shot, in dreariest November. The deciduous trees are bare and skeletal, and the actors barely dared breathe lest the mist register on camera. *Night*'s very first line, then, is a continuity goof, but no one laughs. The peripheral, accidental surrealism of this dead spring suits the film's bleak tone, and this scene's emerging not-quite-rightness: the actors who don't seem like actors, the un-cinematic locale. This is no foggy, cross-festooned Gothic mock-up: it's the Evans City Cemetery in Butler County, Pennsylvania, so drably ordinary that, says Russo, people 'from dozens of different towns' 'swear they recognize it as their hometown cemetery'.[28]

For Johnny, it's just a place of mundane bother. He and Barbara are making their annual drive from Pittsburgh (a six-hour round trip, he repeatedly observes) to lay a wreath on their father's grave. It's a favour to their mother, and Johnny resents it: 'Look at this thing: "We still remember." *I* don't.' This first exchange will be the last in the film that doesn't turn on the issue of survival. For all its offhand naturalism (a far cry from Hammer's expository efficiency), Johnny's grumbling mobilises themes that will explode later: family tensions, generational conflict, the shaking-off of sentimental reverence for the past and for the dead.

Barbara dislikes Johnny's attitude. Ignoring his request for candy, she wanders off to find their father's grave. The radio bursts into life: through the static, the broadcasting studio sounds chaotic; the announcer (Hardman) apologises for technical problems. It's the first hint of the catastrophe ahead, and as Johnny blithely snaps off the radio, teasing the audience, eerie music underlines the implied threat. The score awakens the atmosphere of the deserted lines of graves, but Johnny remains maddeningly impervious, cynically speculating about what happened to last year's wreath: 'I wonder how many times we've bought the same one.'

Thunder rolls in as Barbara kneels to pray. Johnny chides her – 'Church was this morning, huh?' – and lightning interrupts him like a warning of divine retribution. Apparently he's not a believer: 'There's not much sense in my going to church.' At last we feel like we're settling into a good old-fashioned horror film: a graveyard, a thunderstorm, a girl who honours the supernatural, a brash sceptic who may soon eat his words, and perhaps emerge as our hero ... and now a distant figure, shambling through the gravestones.

Johnny rises to the occasion: he probes Barbara's childhood fears, reminding her of when he jumped out and terrified her on this very spot: 'You used to really be scared here.' Little Johnny's horseplay around his own father's grave, he recalls, roused their grandfather's ire, an East European immigrant judging by Johnny's mimicry: 'Boy, you'll be demmed to Hell!'. Romero is digging, too, into his own childhood fears: raised a strict Catholic (though he later decided the faith was 'silly'), he lived in terror of Hell's eternal torments.[29]

Pleased with his impersonation, Johnny slips into one we all know, Boris Karloff, and utters what has become one of horror's best-known lines: 'They're coming to get you, Barbara!' That lurching figure, closer now, proves a handy prop for Johnny's routine: 'Look! Here comes one of them now! I'm getting out of here!' Johnny makes a theatrical break for it, but Barbara tries to avoid a scene. She stays on course for the approaching man, looking up in polite, if nervous, acknowledgment …

But Johnny's words were truer than he knew. Abruptly the man is on her, tearing at her clothes. The mockery on Johnny's face instantly turns to concern and determination, and without hesitation he charges the attacker. Perhaps our predictions were right: a hero is emerging from the scoffer.

As they struggle, electronic effects seize a dissonant chord from the retro music and stretch it into one long, searing squall, starkly alien. The relaxed editing turns frantic: four cuts in fewer seconds as the man lunges. The camera goes wild, jumping between high and low angles, tilting and careening, pushing uncomfortably close as the man's fingers clutch at Johnny's eyes.

Then, as abruptly as it started, the fight is won. The attacker slams Johnny's head against a gravestone with a horribly understated thud: for gore pioneers, these film-makers understand the cruel effectiveness of restraint. And the victor looks up at Barbara, his face momentarily frozen in a lightning flash …

Johnny plays at being in a horror movie … but the ensuing horrors feel all too real

Killing Karloff

Fittingly, the ghouls' first victim dies mimicking Karloff. *Night*'s
opening is an exorcism, liberating the shambling dead from the
Gothic tradition with which Karloff was synonymous: crumbling
castles, gypsy caravans, superstitious peasants – a fairy-tale world
that, even when nominally contemporary, felt remote and unreal.
Johnny's impersonation chimes with his talk about forgetting the
father, prancing on his grave: Karloff was a father to American
horror cinema, and *Night* kills him in effigy, on his own turf. It begins
in a graveyard, like *Frankenstein* (1931), the film that launched
Karloff and established horror as a popular genre. Star and genre
had remained wedded ever since: Karloff was still stalking those
graveyards and castles, courtesy of Roger Corman and Mario Bava.

Karloff's kind of horror had been booming again, thanks to the
stupendous success of *The Curse of Frankenstein* (1957) and *Dracula*
(1958). Hammer and their imitators produced Gothics by the dozen,
and the old Universal films (many starring Karloff) commanded huge

'Baron Boris' (voiced by Karloff) welcomes his Gothic playmates to the *Mad Monster Party?* (1967)

television audiences. But the genre had become kids' stuff. *Famous Monsters of Filmland*, the leading horror film magazine, was unabashedly aimed at children. Toyshops overflowed with Frankenstein lab kits and wolfman dolls. A pseudo-Karloff, neck-bolted monster headed a family sitcom, *The Munsters*. 'Monster Mash', sung entirely in a Karloff voice, hit number one during the Cuban Missile Crisis, a coincidence that hammered home how juvenile the horror market had become, how wide the gulf between the Gothic's cosy quaintness and the enormity and unpredictability of real-life terrors.[30]

By the 1960s' end, most critics were tired of Gothic tropes. Almost every review relished the deceptive familiarity of *Night*'s opening, the way it sets up expectations only to trounce them: 'We feel we've haunted that cemetery ourselves through a stack of "B" pictures,' wrote a *Spectator* columnist, but 'the film has the wit to use horror instead of being used by it'.[31] With that upsettingly bathetic thud, *Night* declares intent: of the contract that a horror film makes with its audience, it will honour only one clause – to horrify. Several reviewers contrasted *Night* with 1960s Gothic: 'fake, cautious horror', as *inter/VIEW* put it.[32] These are the seeds of the modern consensus on *Night*: that it kick-started horror cinema's modern (some say postmodern) phase, and radically, definitively broke from classical models – particularly from Hammer, whose films many write

A popular Aurora model kit, mid-1960s

off as formulaic, reactionary and morally simplistic.[33] This outlook often rests on generalisations about *Night*'s predecessors that can't be interrogated here, but the kernel is true: *Night* is a watershed, in many ways a redefinition of horror cinema.

For Romero, though, cinema didn't define the genre anyway. He has often called *Night* an attempt 'to do a film that was really true to the genre … as perceived in those EC comic-books'.[34] Romero devoured them as a child: *Tales from the Crypt*, *Vault of Horror*. He and Stephen King paid tribute to them in their anthology film, *Creepshow* (1982). EC's horror comics ran four stories per issue – all self-contained, so they had no compunction about killing everyone. Most were set in present-day America. They specialised in brutal, witty twists, typically entailing fatal just deserts for some immoral character, sometimes at the hands of their spouse or child. In EC's default formula (*Creepshow* used it twice), a decomposing corpse returns to exact righteous vengeance. Most stories were spectacularly gory. Before Hammer brought the first red trickle to horror cinema, EC graphically destroyed the human body and put

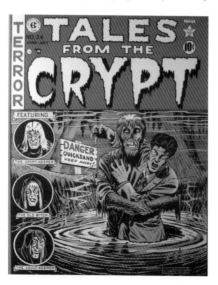

its dismembered parts to hideously ironic use: ersatz baseball equipment, hamburger meat. But EC's sampler comic, *Shock SuspenStories*, interspersed gory cynicism with topical, liberal, realistic stories, attacking authority figures, Red Scare politics, mob justice, war and prejudice. In 'The Guilty', a sheriff panics when the new DA demands a fair trial, not a lynch mob, for an innocent black murder suspect.

En route to court, he forces the scapegoat from the car at gunpoint and shoots the 'fugitive' in the back. The sheriff goes unpunished.

It was a headily rebellious mix, especially for kids like Romero, who had to sneak the forbidden comics past disapproving parents. *Night* offered many of the same ingredients for its young viewers: gore, cynicism, irony, wit, relevance.

Desperation

A long moment of eye contact, then Barbara runs, feet crunching the unseasonal autumn leaves. The music becomes almost programmatic: jittery high strings flit over the inexorable tramp of horns. The sloping landscape and quick-fire canted shots slice the screen into a disorientating funhouse of seesawing diagonals. The camera plunges to the ground with Barbara as she trips and kicks off her impractically feminine shoes.

Hope surges as she jumps in the car – but the keys are in her dead brother's pockets. She locks herself in, and we cower in there

'The Guilty', artwork by Wally Wood, *Shock SuspenStories* 3 (June–July 1952)

with her as the man pummels the doors with his bare hands. It's futile, but this is what makes him frightening: his unreasoning *desperation*. Somehow, he needs to catch Barbara as much as she needs to escape. A rock presents itself with cruel ease and he shatters the window, grabs for Barbara's face.

Barbara takes off the brake: maybe the car can gather speed downhill. Horror film characters often doom themselves by exasperating stupidity. Barbara tries everything we would, but her resourcefulness doesn't get her far. The car hits a tree and she's on foot again, tearing through leafy woodland (this was the first footage shot, in spring) and up a deserted road. Whatever her limitations as an actor, O'Dea holds nothing back: her face and body contort with terror and exertion. Barbara sprints flat-out; her pursuer seems ever slower, stiffer and clumsier – yet she never gains significant distance. It's the authentic illogic of nightmare.

The chase is the first showcase for Romero's furious editing: fifty-five cuts in the three minutes that it takes O'Dea to reach the farmhouse, with barely any repeated set-ups. He shot *Night* with an outmoded Arriflex that needed an eighty-pound soundproofing blimp for scenes with synchronised sound. The budget didn't stretch to cranes or dollies. These handicaps give *Night* a schizophrenic style. The camera couldn't move for dialogue shots, so they sometimes feel oppressively static. When Romero wanted to pick up the pace, he had to cut rapidly between fixed camera positions. But in action sequences like this one, we sense his exuberance at getting the camera

Desperate hunter, desperate prey

in his hands (the Arriflex's erratic speed when running on batteries sometimes, almost subliminally, makes the handheld shots feel even wilder).[35] The combination of out-of-control camera and brutally precise cutting contributes almost as much to *Night*'s startlingly violent impact as the gore scenes do. Romero, a strikingly gifted editor, calls his approach 'almost cubist': he grabs shots impulsively from as many angles and viewpoints as possible and decides later how to assemble the 'jigsaw puzzle'.[36] His frequent disregard for conventions like the 30- and 180-degree rules and even master shots sometimes makes his cutting feel deceptively naive – few contemporary critics perceived how much craft went into *Night*'s 'rawness'.

The montage here is no random flurry. Unhurried, fixed-camera shots convey the pursuer's confidence in catching up. But the shots of Barbara jiggle and dive hysterically, racing through almost subliminal subtexts. One moment she seems inches from smashing the camera (she's flailing, doesn't know where she's going); the next it lurks behind bushes, spying on her: are there others, watching her? And Romero knows when to slow down. A few takes run gruellingly long, to bring home the agonising protraction of Barbara's ordeal: the attacker pounding her window again and again, the real strain on O'Dea's face as she sprints.

Once Barbara makes it through a side door into the farmhouse, he lets the camera sit for twenty-five seconds: we all get our bearings, and atmosphere builds. The music drops to eerie softness. Barbara arms herself with a kitchen knife and explores. The house is no James Whale monstrosity. It's plain, tidy, not old-fashioned, but we see it through Barbara's paranoia. The camera peeps at her from behind furniture. High-contrast lighting cuts the space into sharply defined blocks of light and darkness. The Image Ten lit the house through 'gobos', black seamless paper with shapes cut out. The effect recalls 1940s strategies to pep up cheap sets and monochrome: Romero specifically acknowledges Val Lewton's films, where inky shadows hide unknown terrors.[37]

Barbara's pursuer circles the house, seeking entrance. But there's a phone. As Barbara realises it's dead, her mime-like

Expressionistic shadows in *Night* and Val Lewton's *The Seventh Victim* (dir. Mark Robson, 1943)

grimaces and hand-wringing evoke silent era acting, an odd redolence that returns intermittently throughout the film. It has been over five minutes since anyone spoke or even screamed. McGuinness argued that *Night* 'rediscovers the silent art of story-telling'. Certainly, Romero, like Hitchcock, understands the potency of wordless narrative to absorb viewers, though Hitchcock didn't have to choose between synchronised sound and camera movement.

Barbara looks out of the window again and suddenly things are worse than she thought. Though only seconds have passed, it is abruptly deepest night – another continuity accident, presumably, but it perfectly enhances the nightmare irrationality. And two other lurching figures have joined her pursuer.

Barbara runs for the stairs. Expressionistic lighting makes the banister and its shadows cage her on all sides. She peers into the darkness ahead: something blocks the landing ...

That alien squall sounds again, and a savagely abrupt zoom pushes our face into a corpse's. We're realising that *Night* means to confront us with death more starkly than a horror film should. The face is hideously incomplete, raw and seeping. In this light, it's hard to tell: has rot set in, or has someone torn the lips from those grinning teeth, peeled the lids from those eyes?

Barbara is out of options. Whatever left that mess might still be in the house. She tears back downstairs and outside – where a burst of light dazzles her and us, maybe headlights. A figure lunges from the glare and Barbara backs away: ally or enemy?

Colour blindness

Ben will emerge as the closest thing *Night* has to a hero – and he's black. The dialogue, strikingly, never acknowledges this, but all writings on the film do; indeed most critics think it crucial to *Night*'s meanings. The film-makers have always insisted that they didn't cast Jones to make a statement. Latent Image had used black actors in ads for years. In interviews, they ridicule the contemporary Hollywood tendency to cast black leads only in racial issue films. Sidney Poitier was synonymous with the genre, as star of *The Defiant Ones* (1958) and *Guess Who's Coming to Dinner* (1967), although ironically he was also the first – and, until *Night*, only – black actor to be cast in a lead role not specifically written for one, in *The Bedford Incident* (1965).[38] If *Night*'s colour-blind casting wasn't quite a first, it was still a bold decision (and a bolder role than that offered to Poitier) and the Image Ten refused to mitigate it. Romero remembers that when they tried to sell the film, distributors asked them to 'throw in some Comment,

shoot some more scenes, make a point out of the black guy'. They refused.[39] Jones saw things differently:

one of the beautiful things about that group of people is that it was *not* an issue in their minds. It never occurred to me that I was hired *because* I was black. But it did occur to me that because I was black it would give a different historic element to the film.

He sometimes persuaded Romero, he says, to reconsider scenes for their racial overtones.[40] And while Romero and Russo didn't rewrite to make Ben more 'black', Jones *did* change the character, totally overhauling the dialogue. If anything, he shifted Ben further from potential stereotypes: originally Ben was a slang-talking, roughly physical truck driver ('Ah can handle them two bohoppers'). Jones's version, like Jones himself, was softer-spoken, more cerebral and sensitive.[41] (During the shoot, Jones was a post-graduate student at NYU; many behind-the-scenes photos show him book in hand.)

Continental pushed the race angle. The *Slaves* double-bill encouraged the hunt for topical subtexts: Biberman's film, as Bogle observes, drew 'an analogy between the brutal America of the past and the violent America of the 1960s'.[42] French reviews were full of phrases like 'une dialectique du racisme' and 'le Black Power'. It wasn't uncommon to double-bill horror and race-themed films,

Slaves (1969): many audiences (and critics) saw this and *Night* in the same sitting

Sidney Poitier with Richard Widmark and Linda Darnell, *No Way Out* (1950)

This posed still was used for advertising

Jim Brown in *Slaughter* (1972)

though usually just in black areas: Continental successfully paired *Hands of Orlac* (1960) with *Black Like Me* (1963). Black viewers made up a disproportionate share of the American box office (30 per cent, according to a 1967 *Variety* estimate) – particularly for horror.[43] Val Lewton once tried to win an argument with Charles Koerner by pointing out that *Cat People* (1942) had been a hit; his boss retorted: 'The only people who saw that film were Negroes and defense workers.'[44] Few first-run titles played black neighbourhood cinemas (or 'nabes'), but those that did were often horror films, like Hammer's *Plague of the Zombies* (1966) – and *Night*: one reason why Continental probably saw Ben's race as a considerable selling point.

In a 1975 interview, Russ Streiner recalled watching the film on opening night with an enthusiastic and vocal black audience, and speculated about what Jones's character meant to them: 'I think the black community is looking for a latter day Superman. They find him in SHAFT and they find him in Ben.'[45] In the nabes, *Night* also showed with Sidney Poitier and Jim Brown films. In some ways, Ben is a transitional figure, combining elements of both. His middle-class dress and diction recall Poitier – but whereas Poitier's trademark martyrs sometimes sacrificed themselves for white friends, Ben anticipates the ruggedly independent, self-determining black action heroes of the 1970s. Provocative, ahead-of-their-time lobby cards showed him punching out a bourgeois-looking white man in a necktie (Harry Cooper).

Ben's race was evidently also an important part of *Night*'s appeal for hip white viewers. Hollywood-style message movies were beginning to seem old-fashioned and paternalistic. The sincerity of the Image Ten's colour-blind casting cannot be doubted, but they could hardly have been naive enough not to realise that viewers would read a great deal into Ben's blackness: race was on everyone's mind. Refusing to "make a point out of the 'black guy'" inevitably became a statement in itself, and several critics thought it deliberately implausible that Harry never mentions Ben's race, even in bitter rows.

And then there's the ending: Jones said it was his idea and, as we'll see, it made the film's racial relevance inescapable.

'Don't look at it!'

Ben forces Barbara back inside, brandishing a tyre iron. Once he shuts out the attackers he becomes gentler, but his words stoke her panic: 'There'll probably be a lot more of them as soon as they find out about us.' Ben seems clear-headed, practical: just the man you'd want to meet in a crisis. He asks Barbara about the phone, the pump outside: he has found a pick-up truck, but the tank's empty. But she's transfixed by the ghastly dripping from the landing. Barbara seems to be losing her mind. She starts a hysterical mantra, the same one looping in our heads: 'What's happening? I don't know!'

Ben doesn't answer. Two more of 'them' are outside, trashing the truck. Ben takes them one at a time, forcing them down and clubbing them again and again with the tyre iron. He groans with the effort. Meanwhile, inside, a hunched, chalk-white figure limps almost pitifully toward Barbara. She's too deep in shock to notice. Ben brains him on the floral rug: the juxtaposition of brutality and cosy domesticity is disquieting, and this time we see the ugly hole that the tyre iron leaves. Another attacker pops up instantly, ludicrous in a baggy bathrobe. The camera lingers on his pain as Ben clubs him back. Four more take his place: 'They know we're in here now.'

This unsparing brutality would have stunned viewers in 1968, but it's also crucial to the sequence's effect that it becomes so repetitive: four protracted tyre iron beatings in a row. These attackers are dangerous by sheer numbers: individually they're weak, slow, easily beaten. Reversing expectation, each of Ben's opponents is more pathetic and ridiculous than the last. Killing them is sheer grunt work, involving none of the ingenuity and mystique customary in sci-fi and supernatural horror. What it does require is emotional deadness, highlighted here by the bathrobe man's wretched agonies. Ben doesn't even put him out of his misery. We'll see later how far this deadness can go.

Barbara can't find the right pitch of detachment. While Ben battles, she stares at the figure on the rug. We look back at her from below, perhaps his point of view: more eye contact. But this sickly face seems unmalicious. The eyes still twitch in helpless suffering. Ben tries to break the spell: 'Don't look at it!' But Barbara has seen too much. It's not some medusan ugliness that makes looking at these 'things' dangerous: it's because they're too like us. Ben seems almost inhuman as he drags out the feebly alive body and burns it as a warning to the others.

A queasy realism builds through this sequence, but really kicks in when Ben switches on the lights, sweeping away the expressionistic shadows. That Gothic thunderstorm suddenly seems very distant. Ben ransacks the farmhouse for whatever's useful, dismantling the furniture to board the windows. Barbara's too far-gone to help. She watches a music box with the glass-eyed intensity of a hippie on a bad trip. Strings eerily offset its melody.

The music box is a reminder that beauty has no place in a crisis. Once a home, the farmhouse is now only shelter. Romero's aggressive photography and cutting make this sequence surprisingly violent despite its naturalism, especially on a cinema screen. A drawer hurtles into extreme close-up as Ben's hands clatter through nails and bolts; the camera shoves in to catch hammer blows. Harsh sound effects almost drown the dialogue. The style conveys a certain satisfaction in pulverising this family home, an image that resonates with *Night*'s subsequent assault on the family itself.

While Ben dismembers the dining table, he and Barbara share the little they know in two long monologues. Ben saw fifteen of 'those things' run a truck into a gas pump, while a bigger crowd encircled nearby Beekman's Diner. It isn't yet established that the 'things' eat people, but in retrospect this irony anticipates the mall in *Dawn of the Dead*: the ghouls revisit the diner to consume the customers. Barbara retells, virtually re*lives*, the cemetery incident, fixating on trivia (Johnny's desire for candy) and distorting the truth ('I said "I'm not afraid, Johnny"'). She doesn't use Ben's language: her attacker is 'this man'; 'he', not 'it'. Ben's visibly uncomfortable.

Rehashing the opening is pointless, and in conventional terms the pace is beginning to sag. But this sequence is peculiarly involving. Romero sometimes told his actors to forget they were in a horror film,[46] and here the reassuring vestiges of genre almost vanish. The speeches' meandering looseness helps. Nineteen-sixties genre audiences weren't used to lengthy improvisations, but Jones's brooding performance deviated considerably from the slangy, macho scripted version, and O'Dea adlibbed hers in one take.[47] Romero shoots in long, static takes, and there's no music, just crickets. Stephen King has written that, 'at its best, *Night* ... feels more like a Frederick Wiseman documentary than a horror flick',[48] and these monologues play like oral history testimonials. This is not to say that Jones and O'Dea give particularly

skilful performances: both get rather theatrical. But, as reviews argued, the sometimes-mediocre acting perversely helps *Night* feel *real*, feeding a nagging, back-of-the-mind sense that these are not actors, but actual people under threat.

Barbara wants to find her brother. When Ben insists that Johnny's dead, she turns frantic and attacks him. Ben punches her out. The reluctance and disgust on Jones's face were probably real. He vehemently protested the punch, which he felt incompatible with his version of Ben.[49] Perhaps his racial sensitivity was another factor.

The blow is more shocking because by now we'd expect the hero to *kiss* the leading lady. This lack of romance is another startling break with generic convention that simultaneously makes the film more believable. The same is true of Barbara's mental collapse: hitting hysterical women usually works in the movies, but *Night*'s only candidate for heroine will be practically catatonic from now on.

As shocking as Barbara's breakdown is, it has precedents in Hitchcock: Scottie mutely withdraws mid-*Vertigo*, only to resurrect as a character with whom we can no longer comfortably sympathise; and of course there's the abrupt death of Marion Crane, *Psycho*'s apparent protagonist. Romero has often been likened to Hitchcock, and *Night* resembles *The Birds* in key respects: the mysterious disruption of natural order, the silent attackers who become truly dangerous only en masse, and the fortification of an isolated home against siege. Both films emphasise family, though to very different ends. *Night*'s lack of decisive closure also echoes Hitchcock: *Psycho* finishes with Bates still alive and uncured; the birds halt, or perhaps only pause, their rebellion as inexplicably as they began it. And there are small stylistic debts.

Romero, though, is loath to acknowledge Hitchcock's influence. He worked on *North by Northwest* (1959) and found his methods repellently 'mechanical': 'There was no vitality on that set.'[50] Romero's approach is the opposite: relatively unplanned and spontaneous, with room for improvisation by director and cast. As a viewer, Romero finds Hitchcock's films 'tedious' and 'very, very cold': 'My work, I think, is more emotional.'[51] For all *Night*'s awareness of genre, its transgressions emerge organically from its characters and vision of reality: they simply feel honest, never coldly clever.

Fort lonesome

With Barbara unconscious on the sofa, Ben tunes in a radio: an oversized wooden antique that suits the 1950s atmosphere. Round-the-clock emergency broadcasting has begun, and the crisis sounds worse than we imagined: 'an epidemic of mass murder' is sweeping the 'eastern third' of the country; emergency services are in 'mayhem'. Mainly, the radio frustrates us: over a third in, no Van Helsing or egg-headed scientist has arrived to make *sense* of who is attacking, or why. Reports indicate that the killers may be 'ordinary-looking people' or 'misshapen monsters': 'there is no really authentic way for us to say who or what to look for and guard yourself against'. And crucial information is seemingly withheld: why is the president meeting 'behind closed doors' with 'high-ranking scientists' from NASA? To make matters more exasperating, the sound effects and score increasingly drown the broadcast. Only the gist emerges: 'Stay indoors at all costs'; secure your home.

Meanwhile, Ben salvages timber, boards windows, pushes out a burning armchair to deter intruders. At over six minutes, it's a long, methodical sequence. Ben works silently, as intent on his chores as the camera is on recording every detail, down to the cigarette break. Both seem so focused, so heedless of the audience, that the feel of entertainment almost evaporates. It's like an educational reel on civil defence, more so because Romero deliberately used the 'wrong' film stock (Tri X) to give these shots 'that flat kind of graininess'.[52]

I'll argue later that these scenes tap Romero's childhood fears of nuclear war, but they must also have felt grimly up to date.

Louis Harris, looking back from 1973, identified 1968 as a turning point in Americans' sense of safety, citing assassinations, race riots and sharply escalating street crime.

Somehow, almost overnight, the entire hierarchy of orderly communications in a democracy was being by-passed ... suddenly the streets had become a battleground, no neighbourhood was immune. Life had been reduced to the raw and primitive proposition of physical survival right outside the house where one lived.

Harris ran the influential Harris Survey, syndicated twice weekly in hundreds of newspapers. A 1963 poll showed only 2 per cent of Americans seriously worried about crime and violence; by late 1968, the proportion jumped to two-*thirds*. Just over half said they kept a gun in their home, and were prepared to use it against rioters. Harris surveys from 1971, when *Night* reopened, found over half of respondents fitting extra locks, barring windows and avoiding going out at night. Most felt unsafe on the streets, and many admitted to 'watching out the window for suspicious strangers'. Almost three-quarters agreed that 'law and order had broken down in the country'.[53] This scene chimes with those anxieties: the newscaster announces an unexplained crime surge, a band of 'assassins'; Ben's barricade is like a grotesque parody of those extra locks and bars. He finds a rifle and bullets, the better to weather the siege.

But domestic security is a lonely business. The camera slowly pans around Ben's handiwork: bare walls, ruined furniture, doors that no longer open, windows that no longer see, a house that has ceased to be a home. It's a deep, lingering, desolate shot, conveying not safety but loneliness and entrapment. The radio's chatter only emphasises Ben's solitude. Romero has argued that *Night* preys on fears 'of being isolated and alone, even in the community'.[54] And Ben seems even more alone when Barbara regains consciousness, now locked deep inside herself, eyes fixed on empty space. 'I don't know

if you're hearing me,' Ben says as he updates her. Maddeningly, his words obscure a new development on the radio: '... obscure kind of conspiracy ... creatures from outer space'.

Ben goes upstairs to shift the oozing corpse, leaving Barbara as another story breaks: the killers 'are eating their victims'. The newscaster repeats and rephrases the fact five times as the camera slowly zooms in on Barbara's stubbornly stony face: she refuses to assimilate more horrors.

But she screams when the cellar door jolts open. Two men burst in. The older one brandishes a crude weapon. Ironically, it's his menacing expression that immediately proves he isn't a 'thing': they never look this sneaky and hostile. Ben charges to Barbara's defence.

The newcomers are 'from town', and don't seem to know the house or area much better than Ben does. The younger man is Tom (Keith Wayne, a local nightclub singer), a polite, clean-cut eager beaver. The middle-aged one is Harry Cooper. His wife is downstairs, nursing their daughter, who has been bitten by a ghoul. Harry is respectable-looking but furtive, aggressive and cowardly: he heard Barbara's screams from the cellar but stayed put. 'We luck into a safe place and you're telling us we've got to risk our lives because someone might need help, huh?' Tom didn't help either, but Ben immediately narrows his animosity on Harry. From here on, life in the house will be one long row.

The argument centres on whether they should hole up in the cellar and, in keeping with *Night*'s grinding naturalism, it's thrashed out at repetitive length. Each man accuses the other of stupidity and madness. Harry insists that the ground floor has too many windows and doors to defend; in the cellar they'd have just one door to worry about. But Ben says they'd have nowhere to run: 'The cellar's a death trap.'

As if to prove Harry's point, hands burst through a window to grab Ben. Tom clubs them: the fingers crumble bloodlessly away. Ben tries his rifle, but chest-shots achieve nothing. He aims higher and this time he kills one, establishing zombie films' cardinal rule: shoot them in the head.

Life among the dead

As the body falls, we cut away from the house for our first long look at a crowd of 'things' apart from their human prey, just milling around. One wears his best suit; another, in a toga-like shroud, looks like he strayed in from some cut-rate Roman epic; a female is fully nude.[55] The music drops to a low, unearthly whoosh, and chirping crickets emphasise the hush: the tranquillity contrasts with the shouting match inside. The figures look innocent and ungainly, like babies (as they might, newly reborn). The shrouded one clumsily clutches at a moth. Another (Marilyn Eastman, hiding under make-up) plucks a wriggling bug and eats it alive. It's a haunting image, less because it disgusts us than because it so vividly communicates the creatures' demeaning desperation. Like Ben's increasingly abject victims, they inspire more sympathy than fear.

Even 1960s audiences probably guessed by now that these are 'the living dead' (they might not have, had the Image Ten kept their original title). Everyone now thinks of *Night* as the definitive zombie film, but it never uses the word, and few, if any, contemporary reviewers saw it in that context (the connection only became automatic after *Dawn of the Dead* was retitled *Zombies* in the UK and *Zombi* for non-English-speaking markets). Its ghouls broke so radically from the conventional cinematic zombie that really Romero deserves credit for creating a new monster, one of horror's most popular ever since. Unlike most classic Universal-era monsters, zombies lack a stabilising literary origin. The closest was *The Magic Island* (1929), William Seabrook's first-hand account of Haitian voodoo rituals. It inspired a stage play, *Zombie*, and then the first zombie film, *White Zombie* (1932). Halperin's film, like most that followed, emulated Seabrook's exotica: tropical islands, voodoo rituals, dusky natives. *Night*'s shabby ghouls, like its settings, are anything but exotic: they're just 'ordinary-looking people'. We're less frightened to encounter them than we are to become them: subsumed into their ranks, stripped of individuality, emotion, everything but hunger. *Night* is the first film to make zombie-ism contagious, through a bite, like vampirism.

The similarities end there. Vampires are wily and suave; they work alone. The ghouls are mindless and undignified; they overwhelm by sheer numbers, majority rule. And Romero, crucially, made them people-eaters, always desperately hungry. While the vampire sips selected blood from delicate, erotic punctures, the ghouls bury their faces in handfuls of reeking intestines: a grotesque vision of a society turning on itself, its citizens literally consuming each other. *Night* downgrades the supernatural into grubby materialism. Like EC's vengeful corpses, Romero's ghouls are palpably dead flesh, stiffening and rotting before our eyes (Hammer's *Plague of the Zombies* was the only cinematic precedent). They're the opposite of ghosts, and of religious conceptions of life after death: their souls extinguished, only their carnal husks and appetites remain.

Romero's ghouls have supported various interpretations, part of *Night*'s lasting appeal. But it's worth considering an idea that recurs in Romero's interviews: 'Zombies are the real lower-class citizens of the monster world and that's why I like them'; 'The zombie for me was always the blue collar kind of monster. He was us.'[56] In *White Zombie*, Bela Lugosi resurrects Haitians to man his mill: 'They work faithfully. They are not worried about long hours.' No one blinks when a zombie tumbles into the machinery. It's like a Gothic spin on Depression-era protest songs: merciless bosses, exploited labourers, hazardous conditions. *White Zombie*'s template endured until *Night*: zombies were created deliberately as volitionless slaves, generally to work, whether in Cornish tin mines or as Nazi soldiers. They may scare us, but the real monster is the slave-driver, the boss.

In *Night*, there's no boss: the dead are raised by accident, and their only master is hunger. They still labour ceaselessly and thanklessly, but it's the survival struggle of the jobless and desperate. *White Zombie* emerged from the Great Depression, and aptly the film that redefined the sub-genre hailed from a city still facing a depression of its own. *Night* was not only produced in the Pittsburgh area, it is emphatically set there: those place names are real. Closures and lay-offs had hit the once-prosperous steel town hard. While 1950s America boomed, Pittsburgh's unemployment ran ever higher, increasingly out of step with national averages. The figures would have looked worse had so many redundant workers not migrated to seek jobs: the population dropped rapidly; homes stood eerily deserted. Initially, the Vietnam War brought hope to production lines, but by the late 1960s the outlook was worse than ever.[57]

Romero was raised in the Bronx and settled in Pittsburgh when it was already well on its way down. He fell for the 'no-bullshit town' (his words), while studying at Carnegie Mellon University, and stayed to found Latent Image. White-collar businesses weathered Pittsburgh's downturn relatively well, and prospects were never as bleak for Romero, a skilled college dropout, as for the average discarded steel worker. But he experienced lean times too. For years Latent Image

picked up little work. Romero and Streiner lived at their unheated
office in Pittsburgh's impoverished South Side, and often went without
food for days at a time. The company had a higher profile by 1967,
but most rich clients still automatically chose New York advertisers:
Russo says the Latent Image team were usually 'broke, frustrated,
and physically and mentally exhausted' – zombie-like, perhaps?[58]

Romero has spoken of the Pittsburgh slump as a kind of living
death:

There are all these dead towns, but people still live there, waiting for the mills
to open up again. When you listen to late-night radio, all these devastated,
lonely people call up ... and it's all they talk about. 'We gotta rebuild this town!'[59]

Talk radio figures large in Romero's *Martin*, set in a decaying
Pittsburgh suburb where even the aristocrat of monsters, the vampire,
is now just another struggling immigrant, lucky to deliver groceries.
By then, mainstream films were using dead-end Pennsylvania settings,
Philip Jenkins argues, 'to symbolize a declining traditional America,
an old industrial world of tight-knit ethnic communities falling into
despair and poverty': *Rocky* (1976), *Flashdance* (1983), *All the Right
Moves* (1983),*That Championship Season* (1982).[60] *The Deer Hunter*
(1978) was filmed in Clairton, where Russo grew up, and where the
Image Ten recruited the ghoul-hunting posse. *Night* came first, with
its nightmare vision of desolation and desperation; its abandoned
homestead; its blank-eyed figures, feeding on bugs and on each other.

The vampire's hunting grounds in *Martin* (1977)

The class theme takes over in *Land of the Dead*, Romero's third sequel, in which a zombie army unites under a black, living-dead mechanic, still in his overalls. They storm a snobbishly exclusive apartment-mall complex, slaughtering the white-bread residents but sparing their struggling workforce. *Land* clearly identifies the zombies with the latter: they're have-nots, discarded and disenfranchised labourers-turned-revolutionaries (shades of EC comics, whose revenants brought righteous justice). As one character says after a zombie infects him, 'I always wanted to see how the other half lives.' Looking back, Romero finds similar themes in *Night*: 'that was always in our mind ... this concept of revolution. There's a new society coming in ... devouring the old, and [there's] the old society being unable to process it, not knowing how to deal with it.'[61] But *Night*'s political subtext, unlike *Land*'s, was not consciously contrived, and its effect is far more ambiguous.

Naturally, contemporary interpretations sometimes tried to locate the ghouls on one side or the other of America's political divide.[62] Stein likened these mute, mindlessly consuming hordes to the 'Silent Majority' who elected Nixon weeks after *Night* opened. It's easy to see why his reading captured imaginations enough to linger in interviews and programme notes. The late 1960s saw an energetic, committed youth demand a new kind of America, only to be overwhelmed at the polls by the sheer numbers of the passively conservative; by the dead weight of past traditions that refused to be buried and returned to devour the future. *Night* was finished by then, but its makers, we'll see, already considered the battle lost in 1967. The new president looked aptly cadaverous, like a walking resurrection of Cold War creepiness: he had made his mark in the House Un-American Activities Commission, exposing Reds. Romero's blue-collar theory needn't clash with Stein's approach: Nixon relied heavily on working-class voters, while most student radicals and anti-war protestors (and probably most *Sight and Sound* readers) came from relatively prosperous backgrounds.[63]

But readings like Stein's downplay our sympathy for the ghouls: the abject, misbegotten spawn of scientific misadventure, like Karloff in *Frankenstein*. Horror's monsters are often partly sympathetic, mirroring, Robin Wood argues, our ambivalence towards the normality that they threaten: they express 'our nightmare wish to smash the norms that oppress us'.[64] That wish becomes unprecedentedly palpable in *Night*. Its pleasures centre on destruction: of generic convention, taboo, people, property, the natural order and 'normal' life. It's possible to see the ghouls, as Romero now does, as quite the opposite of the Silent Majority: a revolution, a merciless wind of change. After all, hip critics interpreted the kill-happy bank-robbers in *Bonnie and Clyde* (1967) as heroic revolutionaries, upturning 'bourgeois property relations'.[65] As many young people became increasingly frustrated by their inability to transform America, perhaps the ghouls vented the desire to pulverise society and rupture order – especially as the reality that they assault seems so anachronistically 1950s. Accounts of midnight screenings describe repeat viewers cheering on the ghouls ('Eat them!'; 'I'm a flesh eater!'), and marauding through the streets afterwards, gnawing on bones:[66] fun and games, certainly, but perhaps also indicative of sympathies and desires.

Ultimately, it's no easier to peg the ghouls as 'them' or 'us' than to sort the culprits of Nixon's victory from its victims. *Night*'s refusal to demonise isn't just some abstract, metaphorical proposition: it informs all of its characterisation. But it does reflect the film-makers' liberal outlook. Romero: 'It is very rare that you meet a really evil person, and also very rare that you meet a saint.'[67] It's an innocuous enough observation, but it contradicts not only most Hammer films, but also the Cold War propaganda of Romero's boyhood (on which more later), with its inhumanly bloodthirsty Commies. Much 1960s progressive rhetoric sought to transcend those glib moral binaries. A famous 1965 speech by Carl Oglesby argued that we should not blame a revolution like Vietnam's for the atrocities committed in its name: 'revolution is a *fury* ... a letting loose of outrages sometimes pent up over centuries. ... the more brutal and longer-lasting the suppression of this energy, all the more ferocious will be its explosive release'. But Oglesby also insisted that even the architects of the Vietnam War should not be seen as 'moral monsters. They are all honourable men.' The fault, he concluded, lay with the corporate system itself.[68] This perspective informs much of Romero's work, especially *The Crazies*, a bureaucratic nightmare in which pinpointing blame is impossible. Like it, *Night* refuses to resolve into a tale of heroes and monsters, even an inverted one.

Mister Charlie

Which brings us to Harry Cooper. Just as we're watching the disarmingly pathetic 'things', wondering if *Night* really has a villain, Romero cuts directly to Harry's bald scalp: the cellar argument is escalating.

Critics have praised *Night*'s ambiguous handling of the ghouls, its break from the 'crystal opposition of good and evil in the Terence Fisher manner'.[69] Significantly, Wood, Romero's foremost academic champion, also crucially helped shape a still-prevalent critical consensus on traditional, pre-*Night* horror: the monsters that it exorcises define 'Otherness', whether racial, sexual, cultural or economic – anything that threatens its reactionary conception of white, bourgeois, heterosexual, patriarchal 'normality'.[70] But many critics have found an 'Other' in *Night* nonetheless: precisely the embodiment of that straight normality, Mister Cooper, the workaday patriarch.

Harry's unlikeable personality is another break from cliché: from the benign paternal scientists of 1950s sci-fi, and Hammer's male, middle-aged authority figures. The generic reversal probably felt both surprising and inevitable to contemporary viewers. Studios had marketed monster movies at teenagers and young adults since the mid-1950s,[71] and by 1968 the generation gap was a chasm: 'Never trust anyone over thirty.' Karl Hardman was by a margin the oldest member of *Night*'s primary cast, and his baldness and white-collar work clothes exaggerate the difference. Any even half-with-it audience would naturally side with Ben, the young black man. Harry is 'The Man': middle-aged, middle-class, middle-American, middle-everything; an uptight relic desperate to prove (to quote the emblematically 1950s sitcom) that 'Father Knows Best'. Hip reviewers heaped up epithets that vilified him not just as an individual but as a symbol for a way of life: 'unpleasant WASP paterfamilias', 'l'horrible bourgeois', 'blanc et ignoble'.[72] Later academic commentary has mostly continued in the same vein: the critics who admire *Night*'s ambiguity rarely perceive that it applies to Harry too.

Romero understood that audiences would instinctively dislike the old-fashioned, would-be authority figure: 'he's coming from a different place, so we are all rooting for Ben because he seems to be more like us'.[73] But *Night*'s characterisation is subtler than that. For one thing, Harry is *right* about the cellar. Nor is he wholly selfish and base: he really cares about his daughter. Here, Ben refuses to let him take Barbara to the cellar: does Harry just want to give orders, or does he sincerely (and rightly) believe that he could save her life? Hardman disliked his own performance, complaining that he turned Harry into a 'comic opera' villain.[74] He was too hard on himself: he introduces a note of vulnerability that deepens the character.

Ben is no saint either: though he is more heroic, honourable and charismatic than Harry, he can also be even less reasonable, and seems more determined to turn the cellar argument into a power contest. With the rifle to lend him authority, he refuses to let Harry take any food down with him, his injured child notwithstanding: 'It is tough for the kid that her old man is so stupid. Now get the hell down in the cellar. You can be boss down there. I'm boss up here.' It's hard not to sympathise with Harry's response: 'You bastards!' – bastards, plural, because Tom has sidled over to Ben. Harry retreats into his cellar, insisting that he won't reopen it, 'no matter what'. It's the last power he has to exert, for now.

Tom summons his girlfriend Judy upstairs, and pleads as Harry bars the door: 'If we stick together, man, we can fix it up real good. ... We'd all be a lot better off if all three of us were working together.' His words touch what Romero has called the subtext in all his films: the need for cooperation and better communication, 'the longing ... for people to get together'.[75]

But it's also worth noting that the 'three of us' are clearly Tom, Ben and Harry: women don't count. And indeed, the women in *Night* never do much to challenge Tom's assumption. As he speaks, Barbara slumps in the foreground, staring into space; Judy perches behind her, looking pretty and vacantly preening her hair. Judy didn't appear in the original screenplay, and Romero and Russo only got round to scripting one scene for her, so actress Judith Ridley often has little to do. But it's not just Judy: the women in *Night* mostly just sit around, a fact that

sometimes embarrasses those who argue for the film's progressiveness. Romero has redressed the imbalance in his sequels and, less convincingly, in his screenplay for the *Night* remake, which reimagines Barbara as a post-*Aliens*, tough-talking, gun-slinging action heroine.

If *Night* has any claim to feminism it is by dint of negativity: it presents masculine power struggles as foolish and destructive and it powerfully conveys the claustrophobia and frustrations of the traditional family unit. The latter sinks in now, as Harry descends the stairs. The cellar in fact belonged to the Latent Image office, but it feels convincingly domestic with its heaped laundry, discarded furniture and suitcases awaiting the next family vacation. Harry joins his wife Helen (Marilyn Eastman) by the makeshift sickbed where Karen (Kyra Schon) lies unconscious: a workbench with a raincoat for a blanket. The nuclear family is alone together. Indeed, this was almost a real, behind-the-scenes family: Schon is Hardman's daughter, and he and Eastman married soon after completing *Night*.

Perhaps it's the actors' familiarity with each other that gives this scene an everyday feel despite everything. As with the monologues, the long, static takes and lack of music help. It's almost as if Harry has just got home from work, loosening his tie, unwinding with a cigarette from his wife's handbag. A spat begins immediately, as we sense it always does. Helen digs into her husband's cowardice, self-justifications and insecurities: 'That's important, isn't it? To be right, everybody else to be wrong.' Indeed, Harry gloats over the thought that the others will 'come begging'. It's not a blaring row, like upstairs; it's the quiet, habitual sniping of a couple who were resigned to being unhappily penned in together long before this emergency. 'We may not enjoy living together,' Helen quips, 'but dying together isn't going to solve anything.' If Harry aspires to the role of 1950s patriarch, Helen also embodies an archetype that 1960s progressives hoped to leave behind: the resentful but passive, pre-feminist housewife described in Betty Friedan's *The Feminine Mystique* (1963). She introduces herself simply as 'Harry's wife'. Romero pursued these themes in *Jack's Wife* (1973).

But Helen also thinks Harry is wrong to stay in the cellar: she'd rather be upstairs, with the radio. Whether or not the cellar is secure, Helen, like the audience, is desperate to know '*why* we're being attacked'. And she trusts 'the authorities' to rescue them: 'they'll send people for us or they'll tell us what to do'. Subsequent scenes will make her faith look naive.

Atom-age nightmares and the nuclear family

'The American family is really in trouble', Stein's review proclaimed. Many critics have subsequently argued that *Night* attacks 'family values'. For Wood, it indicts 'the patriarchal structuring of relationships', exposing ways in which the traditional family breeds and represses incestuous desires and murderous resentments.[76] I want to advance a more historically specific interpretation: that the claustrophobic scenes in the Coopers' windowless basement evoke Cold War images of the insular, isolated family; that *Night*'s take on the family is bound up with its 'atom-age' feel, themes and tropes.

Romero remembers a recurring childhood nightmare: droning planes massed above his Parkchester home to 'drop the bomb. Lots of bombs. Occasionally, an announcer would say "Ladies and gentlemen … the atomic bomb."'[77] Nuclear apocalypse obsessed him. Romero was not alone: born in 1940, he belonged to the generation hit hardest by the Cold War countdown to Armageddon.[78] People still worry about nuclear war today, but Romero was at an

impressionable age during the first flush of a national obsession, when America's euphoria about the atom became hysteria. By the 1950s, Russia was building intercontinental missiles, and surveys showed that most Americans believed the H-bomb would be used against the United States in a world war. Those caught at ground zero might be luckiest: heavily publicised tests showed that radiation would spread far beyond blast centres, causing lingering deaths and hereditary mutations.

Mushroom clouds, ruined cities, radioactive mutants: atomic nightmares saturated the popular culture of Romero's youth, and he saturated himself with the culture. He created, he says, 'my own fantasy world' from B-movies and EC comics.[79] They offered refuge from his chronic loneliness but not, at least straightforwardly, from his terrors. EC's sci-fi titles obliterated humanity on a bi-monthly basis. In much atom-age sci-fi, catastrophe comes by accident: a leak, an experiment gone wrong. In *Fail-Safe* (1964, from the 1962 novel), a mechanical glitch sends American planes to destroy Moscow; the President must bomb Manhattan as a peace offering. At best, such tales would have offered Romero (as horror writer Thomas Ligotti has described his own reading) 'confrontational escapism', a fantasy consummation of his fears. Romero even found 'post-apocalyptic'

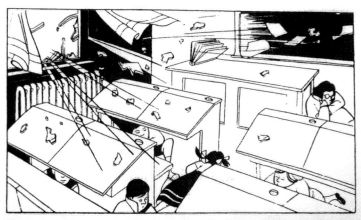

BUT SOMETIMES--**AND THIS IS VERY IMPORTANT**-- THE BOMB MIGHT EXPLODE AND THE BRIGHT FLASH COME... *WITHOUT ANY WARNING!*

Federal Civil Defense Administration, *Bert the Turtle Says Duck and Cover*, 1951

imagery in *Tales of Hoffmann* (1951), his favourite film.[80] For all its newness, *Night* is also a throwback to the atomic sci-fi of the Image Ten's childhoods: radioactive fallout from a botched military project creates the not-quite-human, destructive hordes. Sometimes the influence is more overt: the jarring switch to newspaper-like stills when Ben dies mimics *Fail-Safe* – Romero's acknowledged inspiration for *The Crazies*, which was originally to end with the President nuking an American city contaminated by another mysterious military experiment.[81]

Romero's most terrifying exposure to the threat of apocalypse came at school, where his generation was incessantly trained to confront the H-bomb – especially in Romero's home town, predicted to be the Commies' number one target. No cinematic shocker could match New York schools' 'sneak attack drills', calculated to make children constantly anticipate annihilation. Was it a test this time, or the real thing? Teachers distributed comic books that underlined the point: an attack could come '*WITHOUT ANY WARNING!*'. Like *Night*, the ubiquitous *Duck and Cover* comic (three million printed) was about finding 'a safe place'. Cutesy Bert the Turtle ducks into his shell when bombers come: 'He's smart, but *he* has his shelter on his back. *You* must learn to *find shelter*.' Most schools offered no

better protection than hiding under desks, or even paper. As desperate as the children must have been, it was hard to trust such remedies – especially in New York, where schools issued dog-tags to identify pupils if their corpses (like the ghouls' victims) were damaged beyond recognition. Romero recalls:

we used to get these propaganda comic books in school, where 'the Commies' ... would come into your home and just tear everything up. They'd kill your parents! At the end, you'd pull back for the wide shot, and the whole planet would explode! It all seemed inevitable, like this was a matter of time.[82]

These themes informed *Night*: home invasion, slaughtered parents, deadly fallout. Other connections are more specific. Comics emphasised windows: if you looked through them a bomb's flash might permanently blind you, 'without any warning!'. Another panel showed exploded panes showering huddled schoolchildren. Long after a blast, windows remained treacherous entrances for radiation. For Romero, this must have touched even earlier fears: he remembers his family dousing lights and pulling down shades during World War II blackouts, when again an uncovered window could mean death.[83] *Night*'s terrors often centre on windows: the grasping hands that smash through them, the risky peeks at the ravaged world outside, the desperation to

Prototype advertising banner for *Night*, by George Marino Romero

board them. They're why Harry favours the cellar: 'You've got a million windows up here!' *Night*'s prototype poster showed only a boarded window.

Nineteen-fifties civil defence concentrated primarily on the home. The government's advice was essentially the same as the radio gives in *Night*: secure your home and stay tuned for updates. Americans were urged to build their own windowless, self-sufficient blast and fallout shelters. By 1960, there were estimated to be a million. Private shelters became a cultural obsession. Housekeeping magazines said they were as essential as bathrooms, and showcased designer models. Like Ben and Harry, Americans argued over where to hole up: many took Harry's side and converted cellars; others said garages were safer. Then, there were ethical debates: fathers proudly displayed guns in their shelters, to keep out unprepared neighbours. As Harry says: 'I'm going to board up that door, and I'm not going to unlock it again no matter what happens.' A famous pamphlet by a Jesuit priest asserted that God wouldn't blame you for killing fellow Americans to protect your shelter. Even JFK addressed the controversy. A photo illustrating a typical editorial showed a silver-haired American sadistically grinning as he points his rifle from the shelter door, as eager to use it on the neighbours as on the Commies.

From the *Denver Post*, 15 Oct 1961

WILL IT BE EVERY MAN FOR HIMSELF AT THE FALLOUT SHELTER?

Such articles paint a grim picture of America's *esprit de corps*: if not every man for himself, every man for his immediate family. Once those sirens sounded, your community would be destroyed whether or not a bomb dropped. *Night* confirms this prognosis: selfishness and power struggles divide the characters; they face doomsday in isolation, the TV their only link to the outside world. But this, Laura McEnaney argues, was essentially the outlook promulgated by Cold War leaders. The American government didn't want to pay for communal shelters, so the Federal Civil Defense Administration (FCDA) persuaded the public that nuclear families were responsible for their own survival. Naturally, propaganda put a smiley face on this burden: civil defence became intertwined with family values, as in Project Hideaway, a 1959 media event. The Powner family sampled a fortnight in a fallout shelter, severed from outside communications. Mr Powner emerged beaming. Besides safety, he told viewers at home, shelters enabled 'the integration of the family': 'everyone should build one in his own home'. The presiding Professor concluded: 'shelter life had produced a positive attitude toward the family', by letting Mr Powner 'get to know his children better'. He urged families to unwind in their shelters during peacetime too, relishing 'the excitement of camping out'. Fallout shelter life was the ultimate in 'quality time', uninterrupted 'togetherness' (a keyword in 1950s women's magazines).

With its neatly rowed packaged food, TV and other recreational facilities, the family shelter was both the apotheosis of

Quality time in the shelter, as imagined by *Night* and by 1950s US Government promotional materials

1950s suburban ideals – convenience, functionality, self-containment, familial closeness – and the distillation of the suburban nightmare: claustrophobia, lack of privacy, loneliness, isolation. FCDA guidelines deepened this continuity, extending traditional family roles into the apocalypse: men were to handle the muscle work and dangerous business, while women cared for children and the sick.[84] With the Coopers, we see that Cold War training kick in: Helen cares for the sick child, while Harry takes on manlier chores, like intimidating the neighbours. Like the Powners, they use apocalypse as an opportunity to thrash out pre-existing relationship issues. Bickering in their windowless bunker, they're a rancid parody of the insular family bliss imagined by 1950s sitcoms.

These 1950s anxieties and preoccupations resurface all the more powerfully in *Night* for being expressed less directly than in 1950s sci-fi, and for having been nurtured since childhood by film-makers and viewers alike. Like Romero, most young 1960s liberals grew up with Bert the Turtle: the decade's distinctive spirit was sparked by, defined against, those Cold War upbringings. Robert K. Musil writes:

It was with that awful knowledge – we were not safe at all – that I experienced duck-and-cover drills, and developed an early disillusionment with, even disdain for, authority. In many ways, the styles and explosions of the 1960s were born in those dark, subterranean high-school corridors … where we decided that our elders were indeed unreliable, perhaps even insane.[85]

Psychologist Michael Carey, who through the 1970s interviewed a cross-section of Americans born between 1940 and 1950, found such reactions commonplace.[86] As Musil summed it up: 'The whole idea of combating the bomb seemed crazy; the authorities seemed crazy; the world seemed crazy.' This, for Romero, is the theme of *The Crazies*.

Carey found a universal pattern in Romero's generation, the 1960s generation. All described intense childhood terrors of

Armageddon that they later repressed. With repression came
'emotional numbness': as Carey's former colleague Robert Jay
Lifton puts it, 'a diminished capacity or inclination to feel'.[87]
Jane Caputi interprets the blank zombies as a symbol for this kind
of numbness,[88] but it infects the humans too: there's Barbara's
catatonia, and the detachment required to dehumanise and kill the
ghouls.

Carey found that his subjects were unable to sustain numbness
for ever: in later life, those childhood terrors surged back. Nineteen
sixties and 1970s anti-war protestors rejected the Commie-fixated
politics of their childhoods, but they couldn't shake those Cold War
nightmares. Musil says that, like many of his peers, he opposed
America's involvement in Vietnam partly because he dreaded nuclear
repercussions. Perhaps part of *Night*'s ritual significance for the
midnight crowd was that it allowed them to suspend that numbing
repression and confront those Cold War nightmares, but purged of
their original ideology. *Night* inverts Bert the Turtle's party line: the
government cannot be trusted; the US military endangers us, not
protects us; the insular family is claustrophobic and dangerous; no
shelter will save us. The extent of that inversion becomes clearer
now: Ben has found that most iconic prop of 1950s familial
togetherness: a television.

'Stay tuned for further instructions'

Even Harry can't argue with a TV set, and for now Ben's find clinches
the cellar debate. Harry and Helen emerge and Tom sends a reluctant
Judy to babysit Karen. 'Do this ... for me,' he orders: another bossy
patriarch in the making? Helen awkwardly waits with Barbara,
who's lost in the intricacies of a lace throw, a relic of when a house
was still a home.

Harry blusters in, jabbing weak spots in the barricade. With the
other men fetching the television, he can safely relish the masculine
authority conferred by emergency. He dangles another cigarette from
his lips, Bogart-style; when Helen explains Barbara's bereavement, he

"You bet we bought Motorola TV...we've been a Motorola Family for 20 years!"

theatrically lights up before giving a macho, things-are-tough-all-over nod. When the television arrives he treats it as an extension of his authority: 'Now, you'd better watch this and try to understand what's going on,' he orders Barbara, the unlikeliest person to argue. Ben immediately rises to the challenge of who's the bigger man. 'If you stay up here, you take orders from *me*!', he barks, pounding his chest.

They tune in to a hectic newsroom, where Chuck Craig reads the latest reports. A former newsreader, Craig wrote his own authentic-sounding copy for *Night*. There's been a breakthrough: 'civil defence machinery' has organised rescue stations. Their convincingly mundane locations scroll across the screen: municipal buildings in real Pittsburgh-area towns. The Image Ten hoped that this way at least Pennsylvanians would watch *Night*, excited to see their home towns named.

The broadcast, *finally*, begins to clarify what's happening: the unburied dead are rising to devour the living. As for why, the Establishment consortium – the FBI, CIA, the Cabinet and Joint Chiefs of Staff – won't say. But there's speculation about NASA's involvement: the military recently detonated an experimental Venus Probe that was carrying dangerous radiation back to Earth. This is what *Night*'s audience has craved for the last maddening hour, but the characters are only interested in reaching a rescue centre: their heated discussion half-drowns what sounds like crucial exposition.

The broadcast cuts to Washington, DC, where a meeting on the Probe has just broken up. A phalanx of reporters, led by 'newsman

Don Quinn' (Romero), pursues three delegates: a uniformed military representative flanked by scientists. They can't get their story straight: the scientists insist on 'a definite connection' between the Probe and the 'mutations'. But the army man tries to silence them, his tone sneaky and bullying: 'Doctor, please, I thought we decided that is not proved yet.' Clearly more concerned with military secrecy than public safety, he dodges Quinn's questions, refusing to admit anything that hasn't been 'irrefutably proved'. As his dishonesty sinks in, the Capitol looms. The cameraman is struggling: mostly we watch the officials' backs as they flee public scrutiny; the audio degenerates into an off-mic chaos of contradictions and phoney promises. The soldier bundles the scientists into a luxury sedan and closes the windows against invading microphones. Flags flutter on the hood as the car escapes.

The Venus Probe is Romero's biggest regret about *Night*, and even the film's champions generally write it off as a lazy throwback to 1950s cliché: the experiment-gone-wrong. Perhaps. But it suits *Night*'s Cold War themes, and it's handled unconventionally, even iconoclastically. The Washington scene interrogates a key 1950s sci-fi theme (memorably discussed by Peter Biskind), the relationship between scientists and the military.[89] Here they flee the camera, squabbling; in 1950s films, they usually join forces to rescue the world from invaders, mutations and disasters. Sometimes scientific research has triggered the problem, but science also cures it. Occasionally scientists and soldiers must settle their differences first, and old-fashioned mad scientists occasionally appear; but ultimately

Romero grills the military ... as the Capitol building looms

films like *Them!* (1954) express reassuring confidence in experts, and in the American military's skill and integrity. *Night* thumbs its nose at these authorities, and a wonderful behind-the-scenes rebelliousness energises this sequence: there's Romero's casting of himself as the dogged interrogator, and the decision to shoot on location – within sight of the Capitol, no less – without permission. They got away with it only because guards mistook actor Al McDonald for a real general.

The reality of America's military–scientific collaboration was more disturbing than the sci-fi version: the Manhattan Project, Agent Orange, napalm. This scene evokes science fact more than fiction, particularly the above-ground atom bomb tests that haunted news broadcasts from the Image Ten's childhoods through to the mid-1960s. As with *Night*'s military experiment, far-spreading radiation caused 'mutations': hair loss, mysterious diseases and abnormalities, deaths. And as in *Night*, it was scientists who insisted on the connection, aggrieved that hawkish generals were trying to silence them. The tests fostered doubts that foreshadowed the Vietnam era: that our protectors were dishonest, more concerned with secrecy than public safety. Worse, one didn't know whom to believe: the *Public Opinion Quarterly* found in 1963 that public 'anxiety' about fallout was exacerbated by 'a basic conflict among the scientists to whom one looks for authoritative clarification'.[90]

Such uncertainty haunts Romero's work: he hates to explain away horror. He regrets the Venus Probe simply because it makes matters too comfortingly *clear*: *Night* originally included other, clashing explanations, but the distributor cut them.[91] Romero's sequels and his script for the remake reinstate the confusion. Even here, though, the Venus Probe theory remains frustratingly unconfirmed – and what were the army doing up there, anyway? *Night*'s vagueness also queries the dependability of mass media, especially television. As Romero puts it: '*Night* ... is specifically saying that ... electronic media doesn't work, people don't communicate.'[92] Like many of its transgressions, *Night*'s TV scenes

work both as social comment and as straight-faced genre parody. Vivian Sobchack argues that 1950s sci-fi films like *Them!* and *Earth Vs. the Flying Saucers* (1956) treat television almost as the voice of God. Characters can trust it to explain the crisis, what is being done about it, and what they should do themselves.[93] This was just what contemporary civil defence propaganda said would happen. The family television dominated those cosily domestic fallout shelter designs: a wordless promise that stations would still run, apocalypse notwithstanding; that we can rely on them to keep us safely informed (in *Dawn of the Dead*, emergency broadcasting shuts down for good). Between *Them!* and *Night*, Americans had turned to television to talk them through real emergencies: the Cuban Missile Crisis, and the JFK assassination, watched in the average television-owning home for over thirty hours. By 1960, nine out of ten Americans owned sets, watching an average five hours daily: television had become the nation's dominant source of information, the hub of its worldview.

Prototype shelter with TV, exhibited 1960. The *Life* magazine caption: 'Modern Living'

Night queries this reliance: the characters make a break for Willard because they trust the television – their second fatal error. It wasn't new for films to present television, the medium that threatened to displace them, as superficial, exploitive and mind-numbing: see *A Face in the Crowd* (1957). But *Night*'s approach is more political, closer to the counterculture. It doubts television's ability or willingness to capture anything but 'official', government-sanctioned reality. This Washington sequence dramatises a failure to pin down Establishment figures and resolve the truth. Later scenes go further, satirising television's complicity in state propaganda. *Night* sees television as alternately confused and coercive, which was much how contemporary televised Vietnam coverage felt to young, politicised Americans.

Daniel Hallin, surveying over a thousand relevant evening news broadcasts, observed a general shift. World War II reporters didn't source information: they just rehashed military communiqués. But Vietnam bulletins were 'typically peppered with attributions, often to unnamed sources not all of whom agreed with one another'. Consequently, reporters sounded unsure of facts and interpretations; there was no dependable consensus. America's involvement escalated in 1967, while *Night* was written and shot, and television reporting responded ambiguously, vacillating between Commie-bashing pep talks and more sceptical comment. That scepticism became commoner with Tet, but reporters queried the army's strategy and progress, not its fundamental right to be there. They essentially accepted Cold War ideology: American troops were 'the good guys'. As Hallin demonstrates, television coverage consistently supported the war more than the press did. It needed to *entertain* viewers, to keep ratings high. And it relied heavily on the government for access, at a time when newspapers coined the phrase 'credibility gap' to mock official declarations about the war.[94]

Little wonder, then, that the late 1960s counterculture treated television as, in Erik Barnouw's words, 'virtually a symbol of the "establishment" ... lampooned in hundreds of underground films and magazines'. A 1967 Harris survey found increasing numbers of the college-educated boycotting it altogether, favouring alternative media like folk songs, newsletters, teach-ins and cabarets. Radicals distributed their own newsreels, and North Vietnamese and Vietcong-made ones.[95] In 1970, Gil Scott-Heron's 'The Revolution Will Not Be Televised' mocked the medium's conservative, head-in-sand escapism amid social upheaval. *Night*'s take on television suited the mood, and probably felt increasingly relevant as screenings rolled on through the Nixon years.

The television scenes rub in the evening news realism of *Night*'s visual format. Romero always films the TV head-on, and this change from his usually skewed, careening camera makes it feel oddly extraneous to the main action. The television screen quite never fills the film frame, even though it's the same shape. Romero always shows us the old-fashioned-looking box around it, reminding us of the set as a separate object, insultingly perched between two chairs: he never lets us confuse its perspective with the film's.

'Dubious comforts'

There's more on the Probe, but we can't hear it: the characters are arguing again, over whether to head for the nearest rescue station, seventeen miles away in Willard. A plan is hatched: Ben and Tom will run for the truck, fill up at the farm's gas pump, then drive back for the others. Meanwhile, the door must stay unbarred: Harry will ward off the ghouls with Molotov cocktails. Again Harry is the dissenter: he doesn't think they can get through that mob with a helpless woman and injured child. But the sick child cuts both ways. The stations stock medical supplies, and on television an expert, Dr Grimes, urges viewers bring the wounded for immediate treatment: 'We don't know yet what complications might result from such injuries.' We close in on Helen's reaction: scared for Karen, but furtive too, as if she hopes she was the only one to catch Grimes's dark hint. Might Karen be contaminated, dangerous?

Helen evades Ben's questions and hurries downstairs. For the first time we get a good look at Karen, frail in a floral frock. She's about ten, but Helen talks as if to a toddler: 'Baby? It's mommy.' 'Baby' regains consciousness long enough to utter her only line: 'I hurt.' The scene teeters between pathos and parody, queasily sandwiched between Grimes's speeches. As Helen goes downstairs, the doctor describes the resurrection of a limbless amputee, able only to wriggle its trunk. The image is as sickly funny as an EC twist – more so, maybe, for evoking the cripples coming home from Vietnam – but Grimes's delivery is *Dragnet*-deadpan. The juxtaposition makes us wonder what ghastly fate might await Karen. Previously, children have been almost sacrosanct in horror, but *Night* has betrayed expectations before.

Meanwhile Grimes's words cruelly deflate the Dickensian sentimentality of the child's sickbed. Loved ones, he warns, will become ghouls within minutes of dying: 'They must be burned immediately. Soak them in gasoline and burn them. The bereaved will have to forego the dubious comforts that a funeral service will give. They're just dead flesh, and dangerous.' The speech connects back to Johnny's scorn for funereal proprieties. Killing the undead in vampire films is practically a religious ceremony, complete with crosses, holy water and consoling talk of eternal peace. Here it's a grimly materialist affair: the ghouls are dead flesh; their victims are dead flesh.

In the screenplay, this escape attempt countdown works very differently: there's no sickbed scene, no Grimes, no Judy. It's all about survival, preparing for battle: the characters improvise weapons, while on television the sheriff explains how to kill the ghouls. The scripted scene looks ahead to action. The filmed version looks back, contemplating what the characters will lose: the bonds of love, life itself. As Ben and Tom nominate themselves to run the gauntlet, they exchange a long, almost tender, look of wordless doubt. Melancholy music steals in softly, making their failure feel almost inevitable. Once they unbar the door, the film will become one remorseless chain of disaster and death, but we pause on the brink, ambivalently. On repeated viewings –

and *Night* was famous for repeated viewings – this sequence feels increasingly elegiac, but increasingly, too, like a cruel joke.

That contradiction becomes palpable now, as Tom and Judy share a romantic interlude. She's dutifully making Molotov cocktails from homey fruit jars, like some girl scout turned militant radical. The chore's incongruity highlights how anachronistically clean-cut the couple is. It's not so much their undemonstrative clothes and Tom's short back and sides: this isn't San Francisco, and most Middle American youngsters probably weren't wearing flowers in their hair. They're just too well behaved, too meekly obedient to the authority of their elders (Tom stops just short of calling Harry 'Sir') and, *via* the television, the state. When Judy doesn't want to leave the farmhouse's safety, Tom sets her straight: 'The television said that's the right thing to do.' With death at the door, her main concern is 'calling the folks': 'They're going to be so worried about us.' It's not necessarily retro to care about one's parents, but rebellion seems beyond the imagination of these two: they're like young adults in a film made before rock 'n' roll and teenagers were invented.

As Russo puts it, the dialogue here is 'a bit tacky'. At the start, Tom tells Judy: 'You always have a smile for me. How can you smile like that all the time?' Eventually, worry makes her frown, and we come full-circle: 'Hey smiley, where's that big smile for me?' The tackiness was partly inadvertent: Romero and Russo hurriedly wrote the scene at 5 a.m., about to shoot it after three hours' nap, and didn't realise how sappy it was until the cameras started rolling. Romero, who remembers deliberately 'going camp' with some scenes,[96] seemingly directed it for corniness, and the syrupy stock music makes it almost inescapably comic. All plaintive flute and weeping strings, it's like a wistful *Waltons* episode, with down-home dialogue to match: 'Remember when we had the big flood?'

The end result feels self-aware, deliberately bad, and the parody stings more in retrospect, after the lovers have become 'a cookout' for the ghouls. Nineteen sixties intellectuals could find here, as in the deceptively generic opening, a kind of grindhouse postmodernism, an

invigoratingly unpretentious take on Godard's reflexive subversions of noir, musical and sci-fi tropes. Perhaps the best art-house comparison, though, is to the Kuchar brothers, whose underground shorts were being fêted by the Warhol and MOMA crowds when *Night* appeared. The Kuchars' overblown, no-budget pastiches of Roger Corman schlock and Douglas Sirk tearjerkers – packed with deliberate cliché, bad acting and creaky stock music – were self-consciously failed and ludicrous, but still somehow sincere and moving. The Tom and Judy scene walks the same fine line, catching the viewer between inappropriate laughter and embarrassing tears.

The Fire This Time

That pessimistic music returns as Ben and Tom unbar the door. Judy smiles enigmatically from the shadows. Harry tosses Molotovs from upstairs to scatter the ghouls, then runs down to lock up after Ben and Tom. But Judy darts past: 'I'm going with them.' Her last-second resolve to stand by her man is high Hollywood romance, and we'd normally expect plucky love to save the day. But when the lock clicks behind her Judy freezes panic-stricken in the headlights. Tom is horrified to see her; Ben merely resigned. She climbs aboard and Tom drives. Ben hangs off the pickup, brandishing a flaming table leg at the ghouls: dozens chase them.

Everything goes wrong at the pump. Their key won't work and Ben sets down his torch to shoot off the lock. Tom fumbles the nozzle and gasoline sloshes onto the flame, licking up the truck. Tom makes a

bad snap decision: save the truck. He jumps back in the driver's seat, hits the gas. Ben is left standing. Within seconds the truck is hopelessly in flames, ready to blow. Tom gets out in time, but Judy's stuck inside: her jacket's caught. In another surge of romantic valour, Tom goes back for her – and the screen whites out as the truck explodes.

The couple's shared death is one of the film's more spectacular moments: that's a real exploding truck. But it's also horribly bathetic, even more so than the thud that terminated Johnny's heroism. The lovers are not even killed by the ghouls, who stagger ineffectually in the middle distance, but by the mundane treacherousness of everyday life: gasoline is flammable; clothes catch in doors.[97] In a scenes-we'd-like-to-see twist, Judy's resolve to stand by her man kills them both. Reviewers were shocked and delighted: 'We *know* they'll survive.' Moreover, they die without dignity, served as a hot buffet to the ghouls. The sequence viciously lampoons sacred clichés: courage, devotion. More specifically, it overturns apocalyptic sci-fi's conventions. Even in as pessimistic a film as *Panic in Year Zero*, in which nuclear bombs obliterate most major American cities, it's standard for one young couple's budding love to survive society's collapse, promising rebirth. Healthy, responsible, devoted, Tom and Judy seemed like the quintessential regenerative couple.

The truck dash brilliantly exhibits Romero's whirlwind cutting and handheld photography. But he manages, without killing the pace or resorting to Peckinpah-style slow-mo, to inject moments of eerie lyricism. In one deep-focus long shot, the truck swerves through scrubby fields, pursued by white-clad ghouls. Ben's flame pierces the untimely twilight, and wooded hills roll into the distance, as misty, as incongruously sublime and calmly indifferent to suffering as the Vietnamese landscapes glimpsed behind televised war footage. After the truck blows, we watch from behind faraway weeping trees as Ben leads the hungry mob in a strange dance, torch darting like a firefly. The play of fire and shadow demonstrates Romero's eye for chiaroscuro, which he attributes to his study of Spanish painters.[98]

Watching Continental's shoddy prints, contemporary audiences probably missed these nuances; but perhaps they caught others that the Image Ten hadn't planned. *Night*'s perceived racial subtext becomes pronounced here. There are the Molotov cocktails, indelibly associated in the 1960s with ghetto riots. Over two thousand buildings burned in Detroit's 12th Street riot in July '67, while the Image Ten filmed *Night*. As with Judy, this emblem of civil unrest looks ironic in the hands of Harry Cooper, the white, middle-everything Establishment figure: Mister Charlie comes to Harlem.

The fire motif spreads as the truck burns and Ben flees the hordes. His flaming table leg inverts that quintessential Gothic cliché, the torch-waving mob that burns the castle, lynches the monster: here the monsters are the mob, the man alone. But the flickering flame, the backwoods night also conjure lynchings and Klan rallies, especially as Ben is black and the ghouls all white: exaggeratedly pale and dark around the eyes, like a minstrels show filmed in negative. It's accidental, doubtless – the film-makers cast all-comers to play ghouls, and everyone happened to be white – but in 1968, the image was potent nonetheless.

Intended or not, the racial charge becomes electrifying as Ben pounds the locked farmhouse door. We've kept cutting to Harry throughout, fearfully peeking between the boards at the drama outside. When the truck exploded he ran, and as Ben knocks and hollers, Harry cowers at his precious cellar's threshold. Should he risk the ghouls to save his opponent? He prevaricates too long and Ben kicks in the door. The two of them board it up, momentarily united – and then Ben slowly turns on Harry, relishing the anticipation. He punches him to the ground, yanks him up and floors him again – and again, knocking him through the house until Harry crumples bleeding in an armchair. Ben spits: 'I ought to feed you to those things!' Nineteen sixties audiences were not used to seeing black heroes pummel 'the Man': no wonder Continental used this image to advertise the *Slaves* double-bill. Black or white, we're on Ben's side –

Rioters torch the Image Ten's home town, following King's assassination. *Pittsburgh Post-Gazette*, 1968

but don't we empathise with Harry too, just a little? Don't we privately worry that terror could make us behave more like him than Ben?

The Last Supper

The music drops to a monotonal electronic throb. Moaning in anticipation, the ghouls close in to feed from the smouldering truck. We watch shakily from the passenger seat, as if through Judy's eyes, still conscious as the horde tears her and her boyfriend into finger food. The ghouls sit on the lawn to picnic on limbs and livers. Two fight over a rope of intestine, snarling like dogs. The body parts look grimly real: one of *Night*'s backers, a meat packer, supplied them, and Survinski poured water into the guts to give them squirming freshness.

There's a terrible revelry to this feast, a 'ghastly grasping insatiable' greed that Stein and others interpreted as a satire on American consumerism: 'hands are munched like hand-burghers. (Anyone who has ever lunched at an American drugstore will take these sequences in his stride.)' Romero developed this theme in *Dawn*. Stein's reading of the ghouls as American conservatives probably also springs primarily from this scene, as, perhaps, do other interpretations that hinge on the notion of past devouring the present. These ghouls are conspicuously *old*, certainly older than Tom and Judy: they're silver-haired, balding, wrinkled, incongruously respectable-looking. Again, this was mainly happenstance: these extras were business clients of Latent Image and Hardman, some of

whom surprised everyone by volunteering. But the age gap connects
the scene powerfully to centuries-old folk traditions regarding
bogeymen, those not-quite-human night creatures, unappeasably
hungry for children's flesh. As Marina Warner shows, cannibal stories
since classical times have often centred on generational conflict, the
devouring of the future: Saturn eats his children because he has been
told they will supplant him.[99] Romero doubtless knew Goya's
horrifying rendering of that myth from his study of Spanish painting,
and he captures the same bloody-mouthed, wide-eyed abandon here.

But the scene *can* be read quite oppositely: we've already
sniggered at Tom and Judy's old-fashioned corniness and obedience.
Might they not equally represent an obsolete past, unsentimentally
and liberatingly torn apart? The scene's ambiguity isn't just an
intellectual puzzle, fodder for coffee shop post-mortems: it hits us,
so to speak, at gut level. Those point-of-view shots from Judy's seat
remind us of how uncertain our perspective is. With whom do we
sympathise, if anyone? What is our emotional response to the
carnage: fear, disgust, exhilaration? Are we sad to see the young
lovers die? Perhaps, like the midnight viewers who chanted 'Eat
them', we treat it as a sick joke: after the film became a cult, a *Night*
barbecue sauce was marketed to tie in with this scene. There's a dark
absurdism to this buffet, as to many post-*Night* gore sequences, an
anything-goes outrageousness that recalls those 'sicknik' 1950s and
1960s stand-up *gags* about plane crashes, incestuous rape,
mutilation, war atrocities: anything that would scandalise bourgeois

hypocrites. Lenny Bruce posed picnicking in a cemetery, playing on much the same bad-taste connections as *Night*.

The music refuses to cue emotional response: that throb is blank, unreadable, as if nothing exists in the vocabulary of film scoring to crystallise what this moment means. And why would it? It's a new kind of scene. *Night*'s unsparingly explicit gore – not just blood, but guts, dismemberment, graphic cannibalism – is often identified as a, even *the*, crucial element of its redefinitive radicalism. This overstates the case: Herschell Gordon Lewis had already made gore films, starting with *Blood Feast* (1963); and from Universal and *King Kong* (1933) to Hammer's Technicolor blood-letting, the horror genre had tended to push violence to contemporary limits. *Night*'s leap in explicitness was possible partly because it was released in the two-year window between the abolishment of the Motion Picture Production Code and the institution of the MPAA ratings system (announced six days after *Night* premiered). But this feast scene also feels *qualitatively* new: the noise and fury of the violence are done,

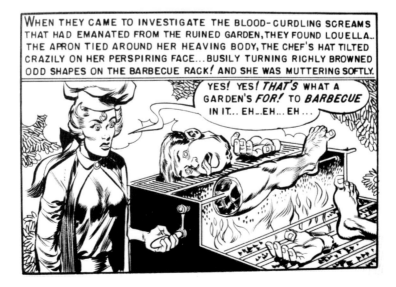

'Garden Party', artwork by Jack Davis, *The Haunt of Fear* 17 (February 1953)

the victims are dead and the suspense temporarily halted, but we linger over the aftermath, the scattered ruins of the human body, like battlefield carnage. It's probably the single biggest influence on a new strain of horror film: the 'splatter' or gore film, the 'meat movie'. The Image Ten called this scene 'the Last Supper', and there's something almost blasphemous in the way it reduces human beings to mere flesh, soulless matter.

Romero managed to redefine generic convention partly because his key inspirations lay outside horror cinema. He attributes the Last Supper to the influence of EC comics, in which human bodies were minced, barbecued, sorted into cuts and displayed on butchers' counters. But perhaps he also channelled a less expected source: *Tales of Hoffmann*, the film drilled deeper into his brain than any other. Romero saw it sixty or more times through childhood: one week he watched it nine times on a black-and-white television; later he repeatedly rented a home-projection print – except when it was out to a kid called Martin Scorsese. Romero says he saw *Hoffmann* as a horror film, filtered through EC comics and fallout nightmares. He singles out the story in which a puppet-maker, Spalanzani, tries to trick Hoffmann into marrying his latest automaton, Olympia.[100] He gives Hoffmann magic spectacles, which make him see puppets as human beings. To set an amorous mood, Spalanzani stages a phoney ball. The 'guests' are puppets, but mostly we see them as Hoffmann does, in human form – only they're deathly pale and dark around the eyes. They move en masse like the ghouls in *Night*, stiffly and jerkily as if rigor mortised. Hoffmann's friend Niklaus advises against his deluded love: 'If you knew what against her was cited ... That she's a dead thing.'

Meanwhile, Coppelius, who made Olympia's eyes, realises that Spalanzani paid him with a dud cheque. He returns furiously to dismember Olympia, smashing off her head with his bare hands. Under a stylised night sky, he and Spalanzani fight over her body, ripping it to pieces. Both men succumb to frenzy, a total abandon that looks horribly like glee. Their eyes are wide, their teeth bare.

They don't stop until all four limbs are severed and the trunk
hurled aside, all still wriggling as in Dr Grimes's anecdote.
As Scorsese, another gore pioneer, has remarked, it's still a very
shocking scene.[101] Romero acknowledges its technical influence on
Creepshow,[102] but *Night* is more profoundly indebted. It's cinema's
first lingering look at a body in pieces (Olympia looks human
throughout), the only real precedent for the Last Supper (with the
partial exception of Lewis's films, which Romero probably hadn't
seen). The puppet-makers' orgiastic fight over body parts feels
remarkably like the ghouls'. The clincher is the incongruously calm
penultimate shot: Cochenille, Spalanzani's bovine, half-human
assistant, lovingly raises Olympia's severed hand to his parted lips –
to kiss or bite? The Last Supper's penultimate shot, again oddly
tranquil, resolves any doubt: a ghoul mindlessly but almost
tenderly raises Judy's severed hand to his mouth and tears away
a strip of flesh.

Night doesn't only echo *Hoffmann*'s *mise en scène*: both films probe the disillusionments of materialism, the frayed edges of human identity. The ghouls and marionettes are frighteningly incomplete 'things', lacking that essence or soul that should define humanity. And where can that spark be found amid the scattered ruins, mere objects now, of either film's lovers? As Polanski asks in *The Tenant* (1976):

At what precise moment does an individual stop being who he thinks he is? You cut off my arm: I say 'Me and my arm.' ... If you cut off my head, what would I say? 'Me and my head' or 'Me and my body'?

Honest brutality

Continental's first impulse was to turn *Night* down, because its gore scenes felt too real, too painfully *relevant*. They watched it the morning after the Robert Kennedy assassination: 'we just said, "Fuck this. Who wants to sit through this? Bobby Kennedy just–" We'd all sat up all night listening.'[103] They weren't alone in drawing such connections. Kennedy's murder, coming so remorselessly soon after King's, prompted a flurry of film industry pledges to curb screen violence. Television stations recalled and re-cut the next season's scripts.[104]

Not so Continental. They eventually agreed to distribute *Night* only if the Image Ten added *more* gore: Romero had to scrape up rejected Last Supper takes.[105] Evidently they changed their minds about what cinema audiences would want to 'sit through' in violent times – and they were right. More remarkably, *Night*'s (and *El Topo*'s) gore seemed to appeal particularly strongly to the kind of bohemian youngsters and intellectuals who typically deplored American institutional violence, whether at home or in Vietnam. Why?

Psychologist Ken Keniston spent a year interviewing peace activists for his book *The Young Radicals* (1968) and found them paradoxically hooked on screen violence. All were raised amid the same duck-and-cover paranoia as the Image Ten. According to Keniston, their belief that a dispute between leaders, 'multiplied a billionfold by modern technology, might destroy all civilization', made them terrified of violence and of the inner violence that catalyses it. They sought to overcome their own anger, cruelty, power-seeking and hierarchical thinking – even as their hatred for injustice aroused their own destructiveness. Repression, Keniston argued, requires an outlet – which is where films come in: the greater the fear of violence, the greater the need to experience it vicariously through art. Between Keniston's book and *Night*'s Waverly run, activists' desperation had escalated: many anti-war radicals (Weatherman, the White Panthers) positively relished the prospect of counter-Establishment bloodshed.[106]

Wes Craven, whose *The Last House on the Left* (1972) owes much to *Night*, offers another perspective on what bloody films meant to Vietnam-era peaceniks. Unlike Keniston's, his thoughts pertain specifically to the kind of graphically realistic dismemberment that *Night* popularised:

The scene that initially decided Continental against *Night* ... and what they watched on TV the night before

gore stood for everything that was hidden in society. Guts stood for issues that were being repressed, so the sight of a body being eviscerated was exhilarating to the audience because they felt: 'Thank god it's finally out in the open and slopping around on the floor.'

Craven saw gore scenes as a way to pull away the veils of hypocrisy and euphemism, to face American violence in all its ugliness. He relates this above all to Vietnam: 'There was a great amount of feeling that, "The worst of it is being censored. … It's time we showed things the way they really are."' After all, the My Lai massacre stayed hushed up for almost two years. It has become a truism that Vietnam coverage brought nightly carnage into America's living rooms: that point-blank pistol execution is the perennially cited example. Hallin, though, demonstrates that television news systematically downplayed the bloodshed. A CBS directive demanded 'great caution' and 'good taste' in showing casualties: 'Shots can be selected that are not grisly … to avoid offending families of war victims.' For sceptics like Craven, the rare brutally explicit clips that slipped through the net were the exceptions that proved the rule: moments when the machinery of censorship and euphemism faltered and home viewers got just a glimpse of what things were really like out there. Bloody coverage was scarcest before the Tet Offensive, when *Night* was made – and, as we'll see, *Night*'s posse scenes also suggest that television shelters viewers from troubling truths.

Craven used a 'reality-based' visual style (his phrase) to anchor *Last House*'s gore in current events. He shot the most brutal scenes handheld on fast, grainy stock, he says, to mimic war footage. The desired effect was the opposite of *Last House*'s advertising slogan: American violence is *not* 'only a movie … only a movie …'.[107] Like many of his contemporaries, Craven learned from *Night*. Despite Romero's fondness for EC comics, *Night*'s gore never feels cartoonish: its drab naturalism was integral to its appeal. Significantly, Lewis's luridly colourful, exaggeratedly ghoulish *Blood*

Feast flopped when the Elgin revived it for midnight shows. That rough, on-the-spot handheld camera and even the monochrome make *Night*'s gore special: they enhance its evening news impact, its connectedness to reality. A *Village Voice* article attributed *Night*'s cult appeal to its 'honest brutality'.[108]

Night's blend of splatter shocks and topicality was richly precedented. Paris's Grand Guignol theatre, a byword for gore, pulled subjects straight from newspapers: a 1904 play ghoulishly dramatised the Boxer Rebellion of 1900, roughly equivalent to tackling 9/11 today. Typical programmes interspersed horror set pieces with grimly naturalistic vignettes about France's underclass, indicting capitalism and bourgeois morality. The taboo-breaking gore scenes fit into a broader attempt to touch raw nerves.[109] To an extent, EC (who once set a story at the Grand Guignol) continued that tradition, juxtaposing bloody horror with social protest.

No single theory can fit all gore fans, or perhaps even the unsettled, contradictory emotions stirred in a single viewer: Craven's and Keniston's both ring partly true. A typically raving *El Topo* review, published shortly before *Night* opened at the Waverly, illuminates by its sheer confusedness the ambiguities of screen gore's relationship to the real thing:

El Topo runs RED, with castrations, beheadings, shootings, and mass murders which make the Sharon Tate scene look like kindergarten fare. … I think the effect … is liberating: breaking down barriers of civilized conditioning and reaching places in our souls which are rarely touched.[110]

Potent tensions register here: the critic's hippie transcendentalism sits uncomfortably with his wallowing in materialist spectacle, and with the Manson reference. But more pertinent is the (now clichéd) assertion that film's simulated atrocities out-do real ones. Such responses raise the question of whether viewers turn to screen gore to reconnect with the reality of violent times or to drown it out. Adam Lowenstein argues that the horror and nausea elicited by

An early, defining image of the war, from *Life*, 25 January 1963. Photo: Larry Burrows;
El Topo

staged violence can shock viewers back into awareness of real-world traumas that they are over-used to hearing and knowing about, that have become 'anesthetized' abstractions: a 'return of history through the gut'.[111] It helps that we usually know film's fictional victims better than we do the real strangers in the news. But perhaps a contrary impulse underlies this *El Topo* review. If we let ourselves pretend that cinema's vivid but phoney violence can dwarf horrors as appallingly real as the Tate–LaBianca murders, then perhaps, for a spell, we can make-believe that those real horrors are illusory too: just another 'scene'. Maybe we can suspend disbelief and belief at once.

These contradictions loom powerfully behind the work of gore effects creator Tom Savini, Romero's frequent collaborator (most notably on his *Dead* sequels) and director of the *Night* remake. While the original *Night* was in production, Savini served as an army photographer in Vietnam. Already a monster movie buff and an aspiring make-up artist, he distanced himself from the battlefield's horrors by treating them as gore effects, figuring out how to recreate the ruined bodies artificially – which is what he has done ever since returning home.[112] Savini both subsumes and enshrines reality within horror cinema, simultaneously bearing witness to the truth of war and wishing it away into fantasy. Both perspectives, like Keniston's, Craven's and Lowenstein's, depend on gore's feeling real, immediate, truthful – as *Night*'s surely does: a dance along the very edge of the line that both separates and connects fantasy and reality.

Search and Destroy

Back inside, Ben staggers from the window. He has been watching the feast – 'fascinated … and repulsed', as the screenplay puts it, like us. The others look like whipped dogs. Talk is fitful. There's no music, and crickets emphasise the long silences. Harry nurses his battered face, too cowed to raise his voice. Ben is still hatching plans, but they're further-fetched than the one that just failed: they could look for the Coopers' car, upturned at least a mile away; or there's Johnny's somewhere, *sans* keys. Either way, it's a trek through

countless ghouls – and Ben is realising, too, that Karen may be
infected, an enemy within. Barbara is more vocal now, and her
zombie-deadpan unmeant optimism ('We don't have very long to
wait. We can leave') makes Ben's scheming sound similarly self-
deluding. The ghouls approach, still gnawing the ill-starred lovers.
Harry watches: 'Good Lord,' he chokes: a line so comically
ubiquitous to EC's gory climaxes that it feels parodic here.

Where can one turn when the ghouls are at the door? The
television – and it's 3 a.m., time for the hourly broadcast. This one is
more polished and confident than the bulletin from the Capitol.
The military and police have been mobilised, and the newscaster cues
a pre-recorded report from a 'Search and Destroy mission against the
ghouls', tantalisingly nearby in Butler County. A zippy montage
follows the riflemen at work, but shows no kills. They're all-American
man's men: uniformed cops and volunteers, who look like they're
enjoying a deer-hunt with their checked shirts, Stetsons and poachers'
caps. Our on-the-spot reporter admiringly interviews squad leader
Sheriff McClelland (George Kosana): suitably moustached and
grizzled, with an ammunition belt slung over his suit, his tie loose
and three Churchill-sized cigars tucked into his hatband. In between
hollering comically macabre orders off screen ('Put that thing all the
way in the fire – we don't want it getting up again!'), McClelland
offhandedly explains the nitty-gritty of ghoul-killing. It's genre-
deflatingly banal: no scientists scribbling formulae, no crosses and
holy water – just make like a caveman and club their brains out.

Walter Cronkite's notorious Tet Offensive report (1968) introduced a more sceptical note to TV coverage

This is the first of two 'posse' sequences: the only scenes in *Night*, Romero says, that he wrote and directed with politics consciously in mind. It's significant that we observe the posse twice, first within the television's distracting frame-within-a-frame, and later off the record. This first sequence bears consideration specifically as television, and more specifically in the light of televised Vietnam War coverage. The wording insists on the connection: 'Search and Destroy', or 'S&D', was famously coined for General Westmoreland's Vietnam strategy, whereby ground forces were inserted to 'clear' a hostile area and then immediately withdrawn. Through 1967, as *Night* was made, these operations were heavily covered on television, usually in pre-recorded montages like this one, following a team through a day's work. Sometimes reporters interviewed squad leaders; sometimes the leaders themselves narrated: either way, the segments usually reproduced field command's party line uncritically. Distressing footage was minimised, and the patter focused dispassionately on the troops' professionalism and hardware expertise, the logistics of 'mopping up' the area. Even burning villages was just part of the job, nothing vindictive. The reports' euphemistic language was purged of moral implications; some was sporty enough to suit the clothes of *Night*'s posse: 'better hunting today'. The bottom line was always the body count, the 'total score', dispensed like football results. McClelland echoes those tallies: 'We've killed nineteen of them today, right in this area.'[113]

Romero and his collaborators were sensitive, by profession, to ways in which language's tone could be modulated to sell a version of reality. Indeed, the Sheriff's and Pentagon's tips sound like advertising jingles, the kind of peppy copy that Latent Image wrote for clients: 'Kill the brain and you kill the ghoul', 'Beat 'em or burn 'em – they go up pretty easy!' The sequence feels perversely routine, as if television is already settling back into accustomed grooves. Casting would have made it more showbiz for Pennsylvanians: local TV horror host 'Chilly Billy' Cardille played the reporter, and signs off with his real name. This 'Search and Destroy' segment, like the ones from Nam, feels false. It skirts the undertaking's horrors, and even its difficulty. Non-actor Kosana beautifully sends up the all-in-a-day's-work professionalism of those televised missions, their emotional and moral blankness. Asked if the enemy is slow-moving, he nonchalantly adlibs one of the film's funniest lines: 'They're dead, they're – all messed up.' McClelland behaves as if he 'takes out' ghouls every day, blithely asserting that it's 'no problem' to defeat 'six or eight' single-handed, armed only with a club – nonsense, from what we've seen. Like the Washington scene, this one was filmed in daylight and doesn't fit the film's time frame, but the mismatch feels right: it underlines the broadcast's irrelevance to the desperation in the farmhouse. With Tet, those Vietnam montages also came to look glibly overconfident. This scene must have felt ever more bitterly ironic as years passed and the war limped on: 'Would you say you oughtta be able to wrap this up in 24 hours?'

Breakdown

The television blacks out in mid-flow, along with the lights, and those eerie shadows return. The power lines are down, like a foretaste of a coming dark age. Outside the ghouls arm themselves and pound the barricade. As glib as that newscast felt, it reminded us of how much simpler things would be if the characters weren't fighting each other

too. Matching shots show the ghouls' hands grabbing tools, orderly as a production line: a table leg, a rock. Romero's framing cuts them into purposeful limbs, obscures their faces and individualities: the ghouls work as one, undivided by ego. And they pack the frame: five to a shot, battering the house in unison. Inside, meanwhile, each character is framed alone, in separate close-ups, unwilling to unify.

Ben drops the rifle in the hand-to-hand struggle, and Harry's eyes light up. He grabs it and points it not at the attackers but at Ben. He orders Helen downstairs. Now, with windows shattering and boards splintering, it's clearer than ever that Harry's right about the cellar, but his wife won't budge. Harry loses control: he gesticulates with the gun, giving Ben an opening to clobber him with a plank. He and Harry share the frame at last, in combat. Ben wrests back the rifle and cocks it ...

This is the showdown we've waited for, but Romero draws it out long enough to taint our satisfaction: long enough for us to recognise that Ben is savouring his power, and that Harry is beaten and defenceless, engulfed by the terror of death and groping for an exit. By the time Ben shoots, it doesn't feel like heat-of-the-moment self-defence. Harry's face looks suddenly innocent as he reels from the blast. Ben's is scarred by shadow, his lips curling in

a cold half-smile. Helen just watches, wide-eyed, like us: anxious for her husband or to be rid of him?

We follow Harry as he lurches downstairs. He's death-white but some impulse drives him. We enter the cellar through his dying eyes: a shaky, blurred point-of-view shot that makes us see things, at last, from Harry's perspective – literally, but perhaps figuratively too. And all he can see is Karen. He stumbles to her side, pathetically reaching out and falling just short: his dying wish, seemingly, to give her some final gesture of love or reassurance. It's a moment overlooked by those who simplify Harry into a one-note, patriarchal hate figure. Life is not cheap in *Night*. It never quite lets us feel comfortably glad, and rarely comfortably sorry, when characters die: not Johnny, the bully-turned-hero; not Tom and Judy, roasted after we've sniggered at them; not the ghouls, pitiful under Ben's tyre iron; not even Harry, the cowardly, bullying patriarch who was right about the cellar and loved his daughter. We're disturbingly half-complicit every time.

The keynote of this final siege is fragmentation: of the barricade, of the human bonds within. Gobo lighting dismembers the visual field, and montage breaks up the space, making the attack's extent unclear. Romero eschews pans, preferring machine-gun cuts:

a broken mosaic of violent close-ups, hysterical reaction shots and lopsided viewpoints. The camera feels like a participant: Romero came so close to the action that Jones accidentally floored him with a plank. There's never an objective-looking master shot. The sequence feels no more omniscient than unfiltered news rushes from a fresh calamity, without cues or commentary to direct viewers' responses. The lack of authoritative visual perspective suits the emotional ambiguity: we don't know where our sympathies should lie. Meanwhile, the music, perhaps the film's most antiquated, ironically evokes the morally certain universe of 1940s cliff-hanger serials.

Back upstairs, Helen flails in a mesh of hands, and a familiar face appears: Johnny's killer. Barbara's expression changes to courage and determination. She grabs a plank and charges hollering into the fray. Her hair tosses almost sexily, music surges, and for ten seconds we believe, or want to, that Hollywood rules will apply after all: that by shouldering her inner turmoil Barbara will avenge her brother and save the day; the brave individual will beat the mob.

Crushingly, Romero cuts straight to the cellar: Harry is dead and missing an arm. Karen kneels over him bloody-mouthed, gobbling her father's flesh. Helen walks in on the queasily intimate moment, reuniting the nuclear family, and Karen shambles at her.

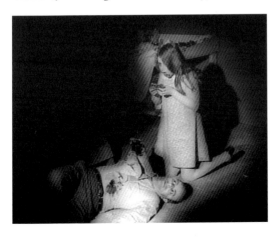

Helen won't acknowledge her husband's death or her child's transformation. She coos comfort as she backs away, ever the fussing mother: 'Poor baby.' When she trips and becomes somehow wedged on the floor, she barely tries to escape.

As Karen selects a sharp trowel and closes in, those subjective shots return, toying with our sympathies: we cut between Karen's and Helen's points of view – and figuratively too, again? From Helen's perspective, the daughter towers like a punishing parent.

We don't see the trowel pierce Helen. It's more than enough to hear the flesh tear, to see her shoulders shudder with each thrust. This scene doesn't aspire to the realism of the tyre iron deaths or the Last Supper; it's heightened, expressionistic as *Das Cabinet des Dr. Caligari* (1920). The blood that splashes the wall is almost luminously black. There's no music, just deliberately out-of-synch screams. They're attenuated, re-pitched and layered into an almost celestial noise: a darkly shimmering clamour of horror, agony and ecstasy. Sonically, the precedent is again *The Birds*, but that similarity reminds us that this climax inverts Hitchcock's. The crisis in *The Birds* forces the family together, reconciles the wayward would-be daughter and the overprotective mother. This one rips the family apart.

It's hard not to see family tensions driving this scene, this sick punchline to the Coopers' domestic sitcom, as Karen turns on the parents whose endless fighting has presumably soured her childhood. The ghouls don't seem to relish violence: the cemetery attacker efficiently brained Johnny and moved on. But when Romero cuts away, Karen has stabbed her mother fourteen times and counting, slowing up the rhythm to savour the feeling of the trowel going in, pulping the breasts that nurtured her. Some critics suggest that this scene is softened because Karen doesn't eat Helen. Isn't it worse to kill your mother just to watch her die?

Night of the Living Dead, starring Kyra Schon

Romero has often revisited inter-familial violence. In *Creepshow* and *Monkey Shines* (1988), offspring kill tyrannical parents to gain control over their own lives. Elsewhere, repressive, old-fashioned parents or parent figures brutalise their young. In *The Crazies*, a father too fearful of the sexual revolution to let his daughter date ('These kids today, they're *pigs!*') ends up raping her. In *Martin*, an old man imposes his antiquated superstitions on his adopted teen by impaling him on a stake. Both sequences are clearly also metaphors for broader generational struggles over changing values (also central to *There's Always Vanilla*, 1971, and *Jack's Wife*).

Does that subtext register here too, as Karen kills and devours her parents? For one reviewer, she represented 'the rebellious young people' who 'have no heart, no sense of right or wrong' and 'want only to destroy' the parent culture.[114] Surely similar thoughts struck other viewers: it's hardly a stretch to interpret parricide as a symbol for generational conflict, let alone in the late 1960s. And Karen's parents seem to embody the past, or at least a patriarchal, insular outlook that 1960s progressives *hoped* to leave behind. It's not just Harry: Helen's refusal to *do* anything as her daughter closes in exasperates us all the more because it culminates her sulking passivity throughout. That review registers this scene's indisputable horror and injustice but perhaps also, inadvertently, its liberating satisfactions. After all, *Night* was championed precisely for transgressing the conventions and taboos of *its* parent culture, and found its cult audience among relatively 'rebellious young people'. Jean-Pierre Putters described the hushed rapture in which midnight viewers watched the parents die: 'Silence please, we're killing!'[115]

Hip reviewers, like Stein, took barely disguised glee in the Coopers' deaths – and maybe that's part of the scene's overwhelming impact. It's horrifying and brutal but more exhilarating and cathartic for it: an unsentimental casting-off of the obsolete past. As Nixon took office and the dead hand of Cold War conservatism tightened its grip on state policy, perhaps Karen's ferocity helped vent viewers' despairing fury at a world that would not bend to the demands of the young. Maybe it's because *Night* spoke so forcibly to the young that Karen, despite speaking only two words, emerged as a cult within the cult, a focal point for the film's appeal. The interviewers from Warhol's magazine asked Romero star-struck questions about Schon. One, Abagnalo, was tearaway enough to have joined the Factory at sixteen; the other, Terry Ork, later became a punk rock promoter. Elsewhere in that issue, *Night* topped gender-bending 'superstar' Jackie Curtis's best-of-year list. Curtis named each film's star alongside the title: *Night*'s, symbolically enough, was Kyra Schon. Many of *Night*'s reissue posters and video covers have shown only Schon's face, pale and dark-eyed, ready to orphan herself. It's also a popular T-shirt and even tattoo motif, particularly at concerts of aggressive, parent-baiting music.[116]

One thing's sure: this time the child is eating Saturn. This is where readings of the ghouls as the Silent Majority or the unappeasable past really run aground. They'll become less tenable still in *Night*'s closing scenes.

Unjust deserts

Upstairs the barricade is collapsing, and a ghoul glides into the breach. Barbara freezes: it's Johnny. Evidently there *was* 'no sense in his going to church': he has resurrected anyway. We'd expect his reappearance to signify the horrors of assimilation: he's just one of *them* now, joining his killer. But it doesn't feel that way. The other ghouls scrum in flailing, mindless hunger. Johnny stands apart: he's suave, barely ruffled by death, coolly intent on his prize. His eyes look victorious as they lock with Barbara's. It's not rigor mortis that makes him reach for

her so slowly: he savours her fear. As with Karen, we wonder: does living death always blank the mind's slate, or can it free life's impulses from reason and repression? (In *Dawn*, vestigial desires bring ghouls to the mall.) Because, like Karen, Johnny seems driven by a special animosity, an exaggeration of his sibling sadism from the cemetery. Now they really are 'coming to get' Barbara, and Johnny leads the way.

Barbara's terror becomes disbelief. She raises her arms to beat Johnny off but wraps them around his shoulders, surrendering, wishing his clutch into a brotherly embrace. Like Helen she can't acknowledge that family feelings could twist into something so hateful. 'Help me,' she whimpers repeatedly, to Johnny more than Ben. Johnny bears her away into the mob, and the other ghouls close in to share. Barbara vanishes beneath the undulating contours of their greedy arms as if into a storm-tossed sea.

The ghouls pour inside; Ben backs away – as bloody-mouthed Karen steals up behind him. He can't bring himself to shoot her. One hope remains: Harry's precious cellar. Karen leads a siege against the door, but Ben bars it shut.

Downstairs the Coopers await company for dinner, still cooped up together in living death. Harry rises to greet his guest, and Ben shoots him three times, wasting bullets. He's yielding to emotion, but not the kind we saw last time he killed Harry. Ben slumps, waits for Helen's eyes to reopen. He only fires once this time, choking down his feelings. But then he gives way, kicking the furniture, wordlessly cursing the cellar and its safety, cursing himself for being wrong and Harry for being right. Upstairs the ghouls are already giving up, mooching lackadaisically around the living room like non-committal house-hunters.

Ironies pile up through this sequence. A girl murders the parents who protected her, pulverises the breasts that fed her. A brother gobbles up the loyal sister who wouldn't give him candy. Ben seeks refuge in the cellar after everyone else has died because he wouldn't. They're like EC horror comic twists bent out of shape, turned capricious and unfair: those 'just deserts' endings can't function amid the moral chaos of Vietnam-era America.

Behind the scenes with the lynch mob

PILOT   I just feel like it's just another target. ... In the States you shot at dummies, over here you shoot at Vietnamese. Vietnamese Cong.

ANOTHER   Cong. You shoot at Cong. You don't shoot at Vietnamese.

PILOT (*laughing*) All right. You shoot at Cong. Anyway, when ... they come into your sights, it's just like a wooden dummy or something there, you just thumb off a couple pair of rockets. Like they weren't people at all.

Morley Safer's Vietnam, CBS-TV special, 1967

We cross-fade to dawn: it's probably the gentlest cut in the film. Birds sing, like the night never happened. Static shots, tranquil as generic calendar pages, show the sleepy farmhouse, the sunrise. Then walky-talkies break the hush. A helicopter soars in, that indelible icon of the Vietnam War. From its cockpit we can't tell if the figures invading the farm are the posse or the ghouls, and that seems to be the point: who are the good guys? Many asked that

Embedded reporters: Steve Hutsko, Bill Cardille and George Kosana

question about the war. Perhaps it's answered when we hit the ground, but not in the usual way.

The posse are 'mopping up', as those Nam reports put it. Uniformed police loose snarling German Shepherds to sniff out the last ghouls. The news team pack up their cameras. We aren't watching the official version now: this is off the air, uncensored. And it's what we'd expect behind the scenes on an 'S&D'. The embedded interviewer buddies up to the squad leader, donating his coffee to the cause: 'You're doing all the work, you take it.' The paper cup brings an uneasily comic, workaday nonchalance to the grim scenes that follow.

This isn't a fair fight: it's a massacre. Nothing about it feels righteous or triumphant: the sky is bleak, the music dreary. The ghouls offer no resistance. They look lost and helpless, unarmed and grotesquely outnumbered. Fifteen men gang up to shoot an elderly-looking female. She gets it like most of the ghouls: in the back, without warning. They're too weak to flee. And they suffer pitifully: one's arms flutter in death; another clutches his face in convulsive agony. The hunters remain indifferent, smugly macho and offhandedly brutal, with the play-seriousness of overgrown boys playing cowboys and Indians for keeps. No one's expression registers the mission's horror: that these are

The National Guard prepares to fire, Kent State University, 4 May 1970. Photo: John Filo

their neighbours, someone's just-departed loved ones, resurrected to suffer death anew. The sheriff cracks a joke as they pass Tom and Judy's remains ('Somebody had a cookout here') and a rifleman (Vince Survinski) half-smirks. The men seem colder than the ghouls, as emotionally cauterised as the pilots in Safer's controversial CBS special – and, we'll see, as reckless of the distinction between combatants and civilians.

But this scene connects just as powerfully with the war at home. Those rifle-toting volunteers look like stereotypical backwater conservatives, the police's natural allies. With their uniforms, paddy wagons, sniffer dogs, rifles, billies and the National Guard waiting in the wings, the posse is the Pigs, the Establishment's strong-arm men. The American cavalry is riding in, like they did at Columbia University, the Democratic Convention, Kent State, My Lai.

This scene's anti-Establishment vibe fed *Night*'s cult success.[117] But though Romero says he shot with politics in mind, chance factors also shaped its meaning. A local radio crew fortuitously arrived in that helicopter to cover the shoot and let them borrow it. Real Pittsburgh cops offered their services (along with Pittsburgh's Safety Director) and brought dogs and vans. The riflemen were volunteers too, local Clairton boys using their own clothes and guns. Kosana recruited them from acquaintances, and it's highly unlikely that

Romero vetted them. Just think how different the whole film would feel if one of them happened to be black – or even had long hair. Very little of the sequence was scripted, and Romero told *inter/VIEW*: 'for most of the footage I really didn't have to do much of anything. I ran around with the cameras.'

But this was exactly what the hip New Yorkers wanted to hear. Almost the first thing they asked Romero was whether the police and riflemen were 'authentic or ... actors': 'They all look intent. Real rednecks.' There's contempt here, not just for the characters, but for the performers, who are assumed to be barely acting. Romero doesn't quite play along – after all, these 'rednecks' did him a favour, but his replies are subtly patronising: 'they were all happy to have guns in their hands. We had quite an arsenal.' Second-run reviews latched onto the posse's 'authenticity'. Ironically, knowledge of the police's cooperation made these scenes seem more rebellious, and Romero's claim to have barely directed made them register as a more deliberate political statement, a point where metaphorical fantasy confronts a barely filtered reality. They became a prank played on unwitting hicks and Establishment figures ('the police and city fathers', as Romero put it), an authentic glimpse of the enemy in the wild.

By then Wexler had staged *Medium Cool*'s (1969) finale amid the real police brutality of the Democratic Convention (one cop hurled tear gas at the camera), and Hopper had shot part of *Easy Rider* (1969) in a still-segregated Louisiana café. He persuaded the actual sheriff and his cronies to improvise, and filmed until they had let all their homophobia and racism hang out. They gawp and snigger at the longhairs, unaware that in cinemas the tables would be turned. Like them, *Night*'s posse became a zoological specimen, a freak show for the freaks.

These vérité posse scenes shift *Night*'s meanings. We may not quite identify with the ghouls but almost everyone agreed that the forces of law and order were worse: deader, scarier, crueller, more ridiculous. Whether or not the rising dead represent revolution, these men are the counterrevolution.

From that shot …

That there is a holocaust coming I have no doubt at all … reaction to Dr King's murder has been unanimous: the war has begun. … From that shot, from that blood, America will be painted red.

Eldridge Cleaver, 'Requiem for Nonviolence' (1968)[118]

Significantly, the *inter/VIEW* writers, and many others, called the ghoul-hunters 'rednecks', though Pittsburgh is hardly the Deep South: the slur was practically synonymous with 'racist'. And racism, above all, inevitably came to mind when 1960s audiences watched this

Police dogs in *Night* … and in Birmingham, Alabama, May, 1963. Photo: Bill Hudson

trigger-happy, all-white confederacy of cops and conservative-looking country folk. They'd seen groups like this on the news, cracking heads at civil rights marches. Those dogs look like the ones that Birmingham police loosed on defenceless schoolchildren during 1963's anti-segregation demonstrations. In 1964, three civil rights workers were murdered in Mississippi by Klan members, a mix of good old boys and local cops. After six weeks of speculative headlines, their corpses surfaced alongside several black men never reported missing: the tip of the iceberg, presumably. It wouldn't have surprised Romero, who grew up reading EC stories about policemen colluding with lynch mobs. The *Night* remake plays up the subtext: the posse hangs the ghouls from tree branches, like the 'strange fruit' in Billie Holiday's song. Nineteen sixties audiences didn't need nudging: as our black hero huddles in the cellar, hearing dogs and sirens, their instinct would have been that he's hiding from the lynch mob, not the ghouls.

Ben unbars the door and explores upstairs. Daylight has drained the farmhouse's atmosphere. It's trashed and deserted: the ghouls' house-warming party has disbanded. Outside, the posse finishes off the last stragglers, and one of the men hears movement indoors. We see Ben from the posse's perspective, warily approaching the window, rifle cocked: he doesn't look like a ghoul. But a redneck takes aim: it's Vince, the one who smirked at the 'cookout' joke. The sheriff leans in to help, Vince fires …

And suddenly Ben is dead. Most reviews spoiled this final irony, and second-run viewers probably knew what was coming – but foreknowledge isn't enough to soften the shock's sledgehammer abruptness. Ben's death hits harder because so little is made of it. There's no music, and the sound effects are understated. A seven-frame close-up shows the bullet knock Ben out of frame, and there's a one-second medium shot of his lifeless body hitting the floor. That's it: there's no drawn-out death scene, no blaze of glory for this hero. It couldn't be further from the lingering, cathartic, beautiful shoot-outs that claim the outlaw protagonists of *Bonnie and Clyde* and *The Wild Bunch* (1969). Sobchack wrote that those films' slow-motion

'kindly stylized death for us; it created nobility from senselessness, it choreographed a dance out of blood and death, it gave meaning and import to our mortal twitchings'.[119] Ben's death is the opposite: as viciously instantaneous as an assassination on live television, with no slow-mo replay to help us understand. 'Good shot,' says Sheriff McClelland. He sounds bored as he intones the film's cruelly banal final line: 'OK, he's dead. Let's go get him. That's another one for the fire.'

Romero finishes us off with a stylistic shock: the image freezes. The last sequence, as the men drag Ben out with meat hooks and burn him, is shown in stills, as wrenching as the freeze-frame that ends *Les Quatre cents coups* (1959). The film-makers printed the shots through cheesecloth to make them coarse and grainy, like newsprint. If we're used to *Night*'s evening news look by now, these shots drive home the ending's truthfulness, its real-world associations – which are above all racial.

Duane Jones said that it was his idea for the posse to shoot Ben, and that he rejected other endings that 'would have read wrong racially', such as Barbara rescuing him: 'I convinced George that the black community would rather see me dead than saved, after all that had gone on, in a corny and symbolically confusing way.'[120]

The ending is more shocking for feeling somehow inevitable: that a black man who has become a leader should be gunned down by, as McGuinness put it, his 'natural enemies, Pittsburgh cops and rednecks'. These weathered stills of grimly purposeful men in rural clothes could be archive shots of a 1920s public lynching, or they could be more disturbingly up to date.

By *Night*'s release, one association had become inescapable. Romero and Streiner heard about the King assassination on their car radio as they drove the first print of *Night* into New York, seeking a distributor. Their first thought was that Ben's death would make *Night* unreleasable,[121] but Romero now thinks that the coincidence was crucial to its commercial success: 'people latched on to the film because they thought that, "Jeez, this is amazingly today"'.[122] Of course, the link with King was unforeseen, but other black leaders had been assassinated before Jones suggested the ending, notably Medgar Evers in 1963 and Malcolm X in 1965, besides lower-profile lynchings. Little wonder that the black audience with whom Streiner watched on opening night responded to the ending's truthfulness: 'You could hear murmurings of, "Well, you know, they had to kill him off!" and "Whitey had to get him anyway." "He bought it from the Man."'[123] It proved almost equally meaningful for politicised white audiences, for whom the civil rights struggle was intertwined with broader progressive ideals. It's this ending more than anything else that made political interpretations inevitable. The *Cahiers* review said that it forces us to acknowledge 'le vrai sujet du film qui n'est évidemment pas les morts-vivants, mais bien le racisme'.

The filmed ending is far more racially charged than the scripted version, in which McClelland regrets the mistake: 'It's too bad ... an accident ... the only one we had all night.' There are no meat hooks, no bonfire. The film omits that line, even though the posse should realise that Ben was no walking corpse: fresh blood pumps through his white shirt when they jab the hooks in. The implication: the white killers know their black victim was alive, and don't regret it.

The meat hooks also evoke Vietnam: American soldiers dragged enemy corpses with wire rather than touch them.[124] Aptly, that helicopter noise surges back as the men tug Ben out, along with a military crackle of walky-talkies. To contemporary audiences, it would have seemed natural for these associations to spark off racial ones.

The lynching of Will Brown outside the Omaha Courthouse, Nebraska, 1919

A 1967 protest march.
Photo: Flax Hermes

Black leaders opposed the war, partly because of the disproportionate
number of black men drafted, assigned to the front line and killed in
action, and partly because they saw the Vietnamese as, to quote the
1966 Black Panther Platform, 'people of color ... who, like black
people, are being victimised by the white racist government of
America'.[125] That's the impression we get as Ben is laid on the bonfire
next to that first cemetery ghoul: they're united by common enemies,
the cops and rednecks, the counterrevolution.

Shades of the war and of racism mingle as the men douse Ben in
gasoline and light him. After hanging, one of the commonest methods
of lynching black men was burning them alive. And in 1963,
Americans were stunned when a Buddhist monk, Thích Quảng Đức,
burned himself in Saigon to protest the US-installed Diệm
government. Romero mimicked the famous pictures in *The Crazies*,
when a priest burns himself to protest martial law. Before *Night*'s
midnight runs waned, television viewers had seen napalm turn
Vietnamese children into running fireballs.

The credits have been rolling since the men produced their meat
hooks, over the film's most devastating moments. *Night* has eschewed
comedy, romance, all relief, and now not even the end titles allow the
audience any let-up, any chance to recover before the lights come up.

Malcolm Browne's photos of Thích Quảng Đức rapidly became iconic

El Topo encouraged midnight crowds to hunt for real-world connections

The Crazies (1973)

Abagnalo described hardened 42nd Street audiences leaving in shock: 'Some people laugh when the film ends, but not because it is funny or badly done. They laugh because they can't believe what they have seen. Some leave silently, looking as though they're about to vomit.' Like McClelland's final line, the superimposition of the credits feels appallingly blasé, as if the unjust killing of a black man is too commonplace to linger over, nothing that warrants a sentimental Hollywood fanfare. But by not editorialising or coercing us into caring, the sequence gains tremendously in emotional power: we recoil from the deadness on the posse's faces, the neutrality of the music and credits. The credits end and for a moment we cut back to action, long enough to watch flame engulf Ben's body. Our hero is not only dead but obliterated. There will be no record of his struggle, no burial or memorial, no hope of justice.

'The world didn't change'

Everyone dies: it's a fundamental truth, but no horror film had ended this way before. *Night* faces the nightmare realisation against which Romero's generation struggled in those duck-and-cover drills: they could follow all the rules, do everything their television said, but they would still die, doomed by the madness of leaders, scientists and generals. And furthermore, they'd *all* die, collectively and unceremoniously: mingled in unrecognisable heaps of flesh and ash. That final bonfire makes us angry at the rednecks, but leaves us too with the sharper sting of meaninglessness, the absurdity of a world that may go up in smoke '*without any warning!*'

But for the Image Ten, *Night*'s ending was also more immediately relevant. They refused to change it even when it meant sacrificing a live distribution prospect, AIP. 'Given the anger of the times,' says Romero, 'if we'd ended it any other way, it would have been hard for us to hold our heads up'[126]: 'I think we really were pissed off that the '60s didn't work, that the world didn't change.'[127] If that's how things looked while they shot in 1967, the Summer of Love, they became far bleaker before *Night* reopened at the Waverly.

Night headed a long run of despairing late 1960s and early 1970s film endings, in which protagonists die and ideals fail not in a pitched battle or blaze of glory, but after the fact, anti-climactically. As Captain America tells Billy in *Easy Rider*, some while before passing hillbillies shoot them for a moment's fun: 'We blew it.'

How *does Night* end, anyway? Romero now insists we know that those Search and Destroy teams won't succeed: 'There's this new society coming.' Well, maybe: the last news broadcast announces that radiation levels are still rising. But it's easier to take that line three sequels on, and there's no evidence that contemporary viewers responded that way. By the end, the ghouls seem powerless, as if dawn itself has dispelled the night's magic. The bacchanal is over. The emotional wrench of that 'everyone dies' ending includes the ghouls, because all of *Night*'s frail characters have souls, even them; and we see ourselves in all of them. Romero's comments probably say more about how he *wishes Night* had ended. And that's the bigger question here: how we *want* it to end. Would it feel less bleak if we *knew* that McClelland's men had overcome the threat, that 'the world didn't change'?

Night's influence is a book in itself; indeed, Kim Newman claimed that *Nightmare Movies*, his overview of modern horror, was 'entirely' about Romero's influence.[128] But perhaps this, above all, is what makes it a turning point. Horror stages confrontations between normality and the monstrous, and most pre-*Night* films are ultimately, at least ostensibly, about overcoming death and monstrosity. From *Night* on, horror more often asserts that nothing will save us, that death and failure are insuperable. More crucially, *Night*'s ending makes inescapably clear that we do not want to see normality restored: normality itself is monstrous; a brutal, painful repression. Romero says that for him 'the most important thing' about horror and sci-fi is 'to not restore order': to leave the world as we know it in bloody shreds. 'Which is really why we are doing this in the first place. We don't want things the way they are or we wouldn't be trying to shock you into an alternative place.'[129]

Night's pleasures come not from restoring normality, but from dismembering it. Perhaps it inverted the horror genre; more likely (as Romero seems to imply) it uncovered what much of it was always, more covertly, about. The only pre-*Night* horror film to enjoy anything approaching its midnight longevity was *Freaks*, reinterpreted in the 1960s as a counterculture film. The self-styled 'freaks' in the audience cheered on the real ones as they vengefully mutilated a bigoted, materialistic 'normal' woman into one of their own: monstrosity, difference won. *Night* was initially sometimes double-billed with *Freaks*, but ended up supplanting it, as at New York's Bijou in 1971: perhaps because its bleaker conclusion rang truer as the years passed.

Night's generic redefinition is inextricably bound up with its historical moment. If the 1960s were a Hammer film, the counterculture idealists would be the monsters: abruptly transformed and possessed, the causers of chaos and enemies of normality. By 1971, *Night*'s ending must have felt agonisingly prophetic. A few stragglers held out, feeble as those last ghouls, but normality had won. It felt more openly oppressive than ever, more repellent for having glimpsed 'an alternative place'. A resurrected 1950s Commie-basher was in the White House: a politician who had announced his retirement in 1962, on the eve of what we really call 'the sixties'. The government's riflemen had rolled in like McClelland's posse to crush dissent. Youth culture's soul had departed leaving only its clothes and records behind, and a new decade dawned, more nakedly materialistic and self-involved even than the 1950s, dissipating the 1960s' idealism into a cynicism and sense of powerlessness that have yet to lift.

Night would be a masterpiece even if we could somehow watch it in a vacuum, as 'just' a horror film. Despite decades of imitations, it remains as suspenseful, haunting and disturbingly credible as ever. Its shocks and ambiguities hit us too deeply to ever be quite assimilated. But a cult, a weekly midnight mass, must also touch its audience's sense of group identity. Perhaps *Night* reassured regular

viewers that even if the world of their naive childhood years had
won, they didn't have to buy into its illusions again. They could
gather while the victors slept to express their disbelief, their
separateness. *Night* became a ritual, an anti-credo, which confronted
cosy childhood myths with disillusionment and destructive fury.
The end credits music is 1950s sci-fi at its dreamiest, but walky-
talkies and helicopter noise gradually drown it. They're the sounds of
the lynch mob, of Vietnam: the brutal realities of enforcing normality.
Night, finally, turns those Cold War monster flicks upside down:
everything that should save us hurts us; every cherished institution is
discredited and bloodied; and normality itself is unveiled as the
greatest horror of all. Sometimes only the truth is powerful enough
to distract us. And if we don't like how this night ends, we'll just go
back to the beginning, to relive the chaos.

We're back at the Waverly, any weekend in 1972. The clock
strikes twelve, the curtains part ...

Notes

1 In the song 'Frank Mills'.

2 J. Hoberman and Jonathan Rosenbaum, *Midnight Movies* (New York: Da Capo, 1991); Glenn O'Brien, 'Midnight Mass at the Elgin', *The Village Voice*, 25 March 1971; Pauline Kael, 'El Poto-Head Comics', *New Yorker*, 20 November 1971; Stuart Samuels, *Midnight Movies* (New York: Macmillan, 1983); El Topo file, BFI library.

3 Misprinted as 'Barbra' in the credits; the screenplay uses 'Barbara'.

4 Tarantino quote from James Marriott, *Horror Films* (London: Virgin, 2004), p. 110. Production information from John Russo, *The Complete Night of the Living Dead Filmbook* (New York: Harmony Books, 1985) and Paul Gagne, *The Zombies that Ate Pittsburgh* (New York: Dodd, Mead and Company, 1987).

5 For more on Continental and *Night*: Kevin Heffernan, *Ghouls, Gimmicks, and Gold: Horror Films and the American Movie Business, 1953–1968* (Durham and London: Duke University Press, 2004), pp. 202–19.

6 *New York Times*, 5 December 1968; *Daily Variety*, 15 October 1968; *Chicago Sun-Times*, 6 January 1969, reprinted *Reader's Digest*, June 1969; *Film and Television Daily*, 21 October 1968.

7 Author's conversation with Elliott Stein, September 2007.

8 *inter/VIEW* vol. 1 no. 4 (undated, 1969); *The Village Voice*, 25 December 1969; on Romero at MOMA, Ronald Borst in Jan Van Genechten (ed.), *Fandom's Film Gallery 2: Night of the Living Dead* (Belgium: self-published, 1976), pp. 81–90.

9 Fran Lebowitz, Pat Hackett and Ronnie Cutrone, 'George Romero from night of the living dead to the crazies', *Andy Warhol's Interview* no. 31 (April 1973), pp. 30–1, 45.

10 Romero interviewed by Sean Axmaker, October 2005, <www.greencine.com/ article?action=view&articleID=246>; *Cahiers du cinéma*, no. 219 (April 1970); *New York Daily News*, 7 May 1971; author's correspondence with Rex Reed, 2006.

11 Interviewed in Adam Simon's superb documentary *The American Nightmare* (2000).

12 Romero, Russo, Hardman, Eastman, commentary track, *Night of the Living Dead* Millennium Edition DVD (Elite Entertainment, undated).

13 Pauline Kael, *5001 Nights at the Movies* (London: Elm Tree Books, 1983), p. 414.

14 *Sight and Sound* vol. 39 no. 2 (Spring 1970), p. 105; *Positif* no. 119 (September 1970), pp. 49–51; fanzine pieces gathered in Genechten, *Fandom's Film Gallery 2*.

15 Gagne, *The Zombies that Ate Pittsburgh*, p. 38.

16 Gary Anthony Surmacz, 'Anatomy of a Horror Film' (a round-table with Russo, Hardman and Streiner), *Cinefantastique* vol. 4 no. 1 (Spring 1975), pp. 14–27: p. 16.

17 Lebowitz *et al.*, 'George Romero', p. 30.

18 Julian Smith, *Looking Away: Hollywood and Vietnam* (New York: Charles Scribner's Sons, 1975), pp. 126–35: p. 129.

19 Alex Block, 'Filming "Night of the Living Dead"' (Romero interview), *Filmmakers Newsletter* vol. 5 no. 3 (January 1972), pp. 19–24: p. 20.

20 greencine.com interview.

21 Surmacz, 'Anatomy of a Horror Film', p. 16; Gagne, *The Zombies that Ate Pittsburgh*, p. 38.

22 Gina McIntyre, 'Chill Factor', *Hollywood Reporter*, 31 October 2000, pp. 16–18: p. 16.

23 Gagne, *The Zombies that Ate Pittsburgh*, pp. 15–16.

24 Thanks to Kim Newman for this comparison.

25 Russo, *Complete Night of the Living Dead Filmbook*, pp. 23, 29–30, 41.

26 Reprinted in Alexander Bloom and Wini Breines, *"Takin' it to the Streets": A Sixties Reader* (New York: Oxford University Press, 2003), pp. 51–61: pp. 51–2.

27 From his liner notes for the *Night* soundtrack album (Varèse Sarabande Records).

28 Russo, *Complete Night of the Living Dead Filmbook*, p. 53.

29 Gagne, *The Zombies that Ate Pittsburgh*, p. 9.

30 On 1960s monster mania, see David J. Skal, *The Monster Show* (London: Plexus, 1993), pp. 263–85.

31 *Spectator*, 20 June 1970.

32 See, e.g., Michael Pye in *The Scotsman*, 1 September 1970; *inter/VIEW* vol.1 no. 4 (1969), p. 22.

33 See, e.g., Waller's influential introduction to Gregory A. Waller (ed.), *American Horrors: Essays on the Modern American Horror Film* (Urbana: University of Illinois Press, 1987).

34 Robert M. Stewart, 'George Romero: Spawn of EC', *Monthly Film Bulletin* no. 553 (February 1980), p. 40.

35 Elite DVD commentary.

36 Block, 'Filming "Night of the Living Dead"', p. 22.

37 John Hanners and Harry Kloman, '"The McDonaldization of America":

An Interview with George A. Romero', *Film Criticism* vol. 7 no. 1 (Autumn 1982), pp. 69–81: p. 79.

38 Lester Keyser and André Ruszowski, *The Cinema of Sidney Poitier* (San Diego: A. S. Barnes, c. 1980), pp. 82–5. Supposedly Poitier was cast colour-blind in *The Slender Thread* (1965), but the film exploits his race for between-the-lines irony.

39 Lebowitz *et al.*, 'George Romero', p. 30.

40 Tim Ferrante, 'A Farewell to Duane Jones', *Fangoria* no. 80 (February 1989), pp. 14–18, 64: pp. 15–16.

41 Elite DVD commentary.

42 Donald Bogle, *Toms, Coons, Mulattoes, Mammies and Bucks* (New York: Continuum, 2002), pp. 225–6.

43 On Continental, horror and black audiences, see Heffernan, *Ghouls, Gimmicks, and Gold*, pp. 205–8.

44 Joel E. Siegel, *Val Lewton: The Reality of Terror* (London: Secker and Warburg/British Film Institute, 1972), p. 40.

45 Surmacz, 'Anatomy of a Horror Film', p. 18.

46 Block, 'Filming "Night of the Living Dead"', p. 20.

47 See shooting script (included on Elite DVD); Jason Paul Collum, *Assault of the Killer B's* (Jefferson, NC: McFarland, 2004), p. 4.

48 Elite DVD liner notes.

49 Elite DVD commentary.

50 Gagne, *The Zombies that Ate Pittsburgh*, p. 13.

51 Stanley Wiater, *Dark Visions: Conversations with the Masters of the Horror Film* (New York: Avon Books, 1992), p. 153.

52 Block, 'Filming "Night of the Living Dead"', p. 22.

53 Louis Harris, *The Anguish of Change* (New York: W. W. Norton, 1973), pp. 168–74.

54 *Clive Barker's A–Z of Horror*, compiled by Stephen Jones (London: BBC Books, 1997), pp. 242–3.

55 Audaciously, so soon after *Blow Up* (1966); she appeared in most trailers and promotional art, sometimes with airbrushed underwear.

56 Steve Beard, 'No Particular Place to Go', *Sight and Sound* vol. 3 no. 4 (April 1993), pp. 30–1; *The American Nightmare*.

57 Samuel P. Hays (ed.), *City at the Point* (Pittsburgh: University of Pittsburgh, c. 1989), p. 18; Joel A. Tarr, *Pittsburgh–Sheffield: Sister Cities* (Pittsburgh: Carnegie-Mellon University, 1986), pp. 58–62.

58 Russo, *Complete Night of the Living Dead Filmbook*, pp. 14–15.

59 Gagne, *The Zombies that Ate Pittsburgh,* p. 75.

60 Philip Jenkins, 'The Postindustrial Age: 1950–2000', in Randall Miller and William Pencak (eds), *Pennsylvania: A History of the Commonwealth* (University Park, PA: Pennsylvania State University Press), pp. 317–70: pp. 325–6.

61 greencine.com interview.

62 See Genechten, *Fandom's Film Gallery 2*, for contemporary interpretations by fans rather than professional critics and academics.

63 A central theme in Ken Keniston, *Young Radicals: Notes on Committed Youth* (New York: Harcourt, Brace & World, 1968).

64 Robin Wood, *Hollywood from Vietnam to Reagan … and Beyond* (New York: Columbia University Press, 2003), p. 72.

65 J. Hoberman, *The Dream Life* (New York: The New Press, 2005), esp. pp. 172–9, 183–5.

66 Samuels, *Midnight Movies*, p. 66.

67 Jones, *Clive Barker's A–Z of Horror*, p. 243, n. 53.

68 Bloom and Breines, "*Takin' it to the Streets*", pp. 178–83.

69 Phrase from *The Scotsman*, 1 September 1970, ironically a rare lukewarm British write-up.

70 See especially Wood's 'An Introduction to the American Horror Film', in Wood and Richard Lippe (eds), *The American Nightmare* (Toronto: Festival of Festivals, 1979).

71 Thomas Doherty, *Teenagers and Teenpics* (Boston: Unwin Hyman, 1988), pp. 142–78.

72 *Sight and Sound*, *Positif*.

73 Jones, *Clive Barker's A–Z of Horror*, p. 243.

74 Surmacz, 'Anatomy of a Horror Film', p. 19; Elite DVD commentary.

75 Dan Yakir, 'Knight after Knight with George Romero', *American Film* (May 1981), pp. 42–5, 69: p. 43.

76 Wood, *Hollywood from Vietnam to Reagan*, pp. 102–4.

77 Gagne, *The Zombies that Ate Pittsburgh,* p. 11.

78 This section draws on too many sources to list, but valuable overviews include Allan M. Winkler, *Life under a Cloud* (New York: Oxford University Press, 1993) and Kenneth D. Rose, *One Nation Underground* (New York: New York University Press, 2001).

79 Yakir, 'Knight after Knight', p. 45.

80 Interview with Romero included on *Tales of Hoffmann* DVD (The Criterion Collection, 2005).

81 Tony Scott, 'Romero: An Interview', *Cinefantastique* vol. 2 no. 3 (Winter 1973), pp. 8–15.

82 Gagne, *The Zombies that Ate Pittsburgh*, pp. 9–11; *Tales of Hoffmann* interview.

83 Gagne, *The Zombies that Ate Pittsburgh*, p. 11.

84 On civil defence and family values, see Laura McEnaney, *Civil Defense Begins at Home* (Princeton: Princeton University Press, 2000), esp. pp. 68–80; on suburbia, see Elaine Tyler May, *Homeward Bound: American Families in the Cold War Era* (New York: Basic Books, 1988), pp. 169–82.

85 Robert K. Musil, 'Growing up nuclear', *The Bulletin of the Atomic Scientists* vol. 38 no. 1 (January 1982), p. 19.

86 Robert Jay Lifton, 'The prevention of Nuclear War', *The Bulletin of the Atomic Scientists* vol. 36 no. 8 (October 1980), pp. 38–43: p. 43.

87 Ibid., p. 43.

88 Jane Caputi, 'Films of the Nuclear Age', *Journal of Popular Film & Television* vol. 16 no. 3 (Autumn 1988), pp. 100–7.

89 Peter Biskind, *Seeing is Believing* (London: Bloomsbury, 2001), pp. 99–159.

90 Winkler, *Life under a Cloud*, pp. 101–2.

91 greencine.com interview.

92 Jones, *Clive Barker's A–Z of Horror*, p. 243.

93 Vivian Sobchack, *Screening Space* (New Brunswick, NJ: Rutgers University Press, 1987), pp. 187–92.

94 Daniel C. Hallin, *The 'Uncensored War': The Media and Vietnam* (New York: Oxford University Press, 1986), esp. pp. 6–7, 122, 160–74.

95 Erik Barnouw, *Tube of Plenty: The Evolution of American Television* (New York: Oxford University Press, 1975), pp. 391–6.

96 Block, 'Filming "Night of the Living Dead"', p. 20.

97 Dillard argues that *Night* is ultimately about 'the danger of the ordinary world itself': R. H. W. Dillard, '*Night of the Living Dead*: It's not like just a wind that's passing through', in Waller, *American Horrors*, pp. 14–29.

98 Scott, 'Romero: An Interview', p. 10.

99 Marina Warner, *No Go the Boogeyman* (New York: Farrar, Straus and Giroux, 1998), pp. 23–77.

100 *Tales of Hoffmann* DVD interview.

101 Scorsese's commentary track, *Tales of Hoffmann* DVD.

102 *Tales of Hoffmann* DVD interview.

103 Lebowitz *et al.*, 'George Romero', p. 31.

104 Barnouw, *Tube of Plenty*, p. 415.

105 Scott, 'Romero: An Interview', p. 11.

106 Ken Keniston, *Young Radicals*, esp. pp. 247–56.

107 David A. Szulkin, *Wes Craven's* Last House on the Left (Guildford: FAB Press, 2000), pp. 15, 47–8, 80. Adam Lowenstein connects *Last House* with contemporary realities, particularly Kent State, in *Shocking Representation* (New York: Columbia University Press, 2005).

108 *The Village Voice*, 17 July 1971.

109 Richard J. Hand and Michael Wilson, *Grand-Guignol: The French Theatre of Horror* (Exeter: University of Exeter Press, 2002), esp. pp. 3–9.

110 Ken Rudolph, *Los Angeles Free Press*, 23 April 1971.

111 Lowenstein, *Shocking Representation*, esp. pp. 46–8.

112 *The American Nightmare*; 'The Dead Walk' documentary, included on *Night of the Living Dead* (1990) DVD (Columbia Pictures, 1999).

113 Hallin, *The 'Uncensored War'*, pp. 135–45.

114 Quoted in Matt Becker, 'A Point of Little Hope', *The Velvet Light Trap* no. 57 (Spring 2006), pp. 42–59: p. 52.

115 Genechten, *Fandom's Film Gallery 2*, pp. 71–2.

116 See the tattoo gallery at Kyra Schon's website, <www.ghoulnextdoor.com.>

117 Compare *Bonnie and Clyde*'s ending, of which a contemporary reviewer wrote: 'The audience really gets angry when the anonymous Minions of Bourgeois Order blast down the Blythe Spirit of the Revolution'– Hoberman, *The Dream Life*, p. 183.

118 Bloom and Breines, *"Takin' it to the Streets"*, pp. 130–2.

119 Vivian Sobchack, 'The Violent Dance'(1974), in Stephen Price (ed.), *Screening Violence* (London: Athlone Press, 2000), pp. 110–19: p. 114.

120 Ferrante, 'Farewell to Duane Jones', p. 16.

121 Surmacz, 'Anatomy of a Horror Film', p. 19.

122 greencine.com interview.

123 Surmacz, 'Anatomy of a Horror Film', p. 18.

124 Described by Savini, *The American Nightmare*.

125 Wallace Terry, 'Bringing the War Home', *Black Scholar* vol. 2 no. 3 (1970), pp. 6–18; Bloom and Breines, *"Takin' it to the Streets"*, pp. 125–8; see pp. 186–91 for Martin Luther King on Vietnam.

126 *Night of the Living Dead 25th Anniversary Documentary*, in the *Trilogy of the Dead* DVD set (Anchor Bay UK, 2004).

127 Romero interviewed by Ryan Rotten, <www.moviesonline.ca/movienews_1216.html>.

128 Kim Newman, *Nightmare Movies* (NY: Harmony Books, 1988), p. xii.

129 greencine.com interview; Jones, *Clive Barker's A–Z of Horror*, pp. 245–6.

Credits

Night of the Living Dead
USA 1968

Directed by
George A. Romero
Produced by
Russell W. Streiner
Karl Hardman
Screenplay by
John Russo
George A. Romero
Photographed by
The Latent Image, Inc.
[i.e. George A. Romero]

©1968. Image Ten, Inc.
Production Company
An Image Ten production

Lighting Supervisor
Joseph Unitas
Production Director
Vincent Survinski
Production Manager
George Kosana
Script Coordination
Jacqueline Streiner
Continuity
Betty Ellen Haughey
Special Effects
Regis Survinski
Tony Pantanello
Props
Charles O'Dato
Make-up
Hardman Assoc., Inc.
[i.e. Karl Hardman
Marilyn Eastman]
Hairstyles
Bruce Capristo

Title Sequence
The Animators
Sound Engineers
Gary R. Streiner
Marshall Booth
Laboratory
WRS Motion Picture Lab

uncredited
Editor
George A. Romero
Sound Effects
Karl Hardman
Marilyn Eastman
Music
Capitol Hi-Q Library

CAST
Duane Jones
Ben
Judith O'Dea
Barbara
Karl Hardman
Harry Cooper
Marilyn Eastman
Helen Cooper
Keith Wayne
Tom
Judith Ridley
Judy
with
Kyra Schon
Karen Cooper
Charles Craig
tv newscaster/ghoul/
voice of radio newscaster
Bill Heinzman
[Hinzman]
cemetery ghoul
George Kosana
Sheriff McClelland

Frank Doak
Doctor Grimes, scientist
Bill 'Chilly Billy' Cardille
Bill Cardille, field
reporter
A. C. McDonald
Washington general
and
Samuel R. Solito
Mark Ricci
Lee Hartman
Jack Givens
R. J. [Rudy] Ricci
Paula Richards
John Simpson
Herbert Summer
Richard Ricci
William Burchinal
Ross Harris
Al Croft
Jason Richards
Dave James
Sharon Carroll
William Mogush
Steve Hutsko
Joann Michaels
Phillip Smith
Ella Mae Smith
Randy Burr

uncredited
Russell Streiner
Johnny
George A. Romero
Don Quinn, newsman
John Russo
army driver/ghouls
Vincent Survinski
Vince, posse gunman

Produced through the facilities of The Latent Image, Inc., and Hardman Associates, Inc. (Pittsburgh, PA)

Special thanks to WIIC-TV (Pittsburgh), KQV-RADIO (Pittsburgh) and the Pittsburgh Police Department

Production Details

Filmed from June to December 1967 in Pittsburgh, Washington, DC, Evans City and other Pennsylvania locations (35mm, black and white, mono, 1.33:1)

Working Titles

Night of the Flesh Eaters
Night of Anubis

US theatrical release by Continental Distributing, Inc. (Pittsburgh opening on 1 October 1968). Running time: 96 minutes

Credits compiled by Julian Grainger

List of Illustrations

While considerable effort has been made to identify the copyright holders this has not been possible in all cases. We apologise for any apparent negligence and any omissions or corrections brought to our attention will be remedied in future editions.

Night of the Living Dead, Image Ten; p. 10 – *The Last Man on Earth*, Produzioni La Regina/American International Productions; p. 22 – Vietnam Execution, © AP/PA Photos; p. 28 – *Invisible Invaders*, Premium Pictures; p. 34 – *Mad Monster Party?*, Rankin-Bass Productions; p. 40 – *The Seventh Victim*, © RKO Radio Pictures; p. 43 – *Slaves*, Slaves Company/Theatre Guild Films/Walter Reade Organisation; p. 44 – *No Way Out*, © Twentieth Century-Fox Film Corporation; *Slaughter*, American International Productions/Slaughter United Partnership; p. 58 – *Martin*, Braddock Associates/Laurel Entertainment; p. 89 – *Tales of Hoffmann*, Michael Powell and Emeric Pressburger/British Lion Film Corporation; p. 94 – *El Topo*, Abkco Films; p. 111 – Birmingham Protest, © AP/PA Photos; p. 117 – Vietnam Monk Protest, © AP/PA Photos; *The Crazies*, © Pittsburgh Films.